The Night We First Met

A MYSTIC JOURNEY

KAVINDRA

Second Edition 2007

FINALIST
National Indie Excellence Awards 2007

First Printing Limited Signed and Numbered Edition 2006
©Jeffrey Armstrong 2006
All Rights Reserved
www.JeffreyArmstrong.com

Poems may be used or reproduced with the written permission of the
author providing the author's name remains with the poem at all times.
For permission contact 1-866-872-6224 or vasa108@telus.net
Published by VASA Publishing
VASA - Vedic Academy of Sciences & Arts

Cover & Text Design Sandi Graham & Richelle Jarrell
Graphics Consulting Jane Weitzel & Samantha Reynolds
Front Cover Photo by © Annet2005
Back Cover Art © Holly Kuchera Dreamstime.com

To: Miriam

may the Divine Couple
include you in their circle.

Author's Signature: Jeffrey Armstrong • Kavindra

Dee 12, 2007
Date:

Voncouver, Canada
City:

Jeffrey Armstrong

3

Dedication

I dedicate this book to my beloved Guru Maharaja

His Divine Grace A. C. Bhaktivedanta Swami Prabhupada

who planted the seed of loving devotion to the Divine Couple

within my heart almost forty years ago.

Acknowledgements

Our modern world is dangerously close to losing many things. One of these is poetry, the sacred use of language. I say this as one who has remained committed to writing poetry and believing in its value for the last 48 years. There is an ancient saying: "Don't write poetry unless you'll die if you don't." I certainly would have. So it is, that for an endangered species like myself, those who have been supportive of or encouraging about poetry in my life, are deserving of some appreciation for their kindness and love.

My special thanks go to Robin and Paul Noll, Michael Cassidy, Ron Marinelli, Mark Muchnick, Paul Hansen, Jennifer Taylor, Guenevere Armstrong, Keshava Smith, Amy Armstrong, Avar Laland, Noel King, Donald Nichole, Charles Selberg, Thomas Barquee, Pete McCormack, Samantha Reynolds, Petrula Vrontikis, Pat Rekert, Mike Van Kuyk, Jane Weitzel, Carmen Everall, Hari Singh Khalsa, Paul Young, Eddie Vaillancourt, Rik Goltz, Hemalayaa, Sonja Picard, Sarala Thompson and the many students, friends and family around the world who made publishing this book possible.

I would like to offer special thanks to Richelle Jarrell, who has been a student, friend, editor and proof-reader and who has helped in a myriad of ways to make this book a reality.

Most especially, I would like to thank my partner, friend and beloved Sandi Graham. The first thing to say is that when we first met, she promised that these poems would be published while I am still alive. No one has ever taken such a personal interest in bringing my visions, dreams, words and teachings to the world as she has or worked so hard at making it a reality. She also designed the book, nurtured it into being and stayed up many late nights shaping it and giving it birth. She is my muse, best friend, life partner and fellow lover in the Divine.

May all of you dear friends be blessed always with an eternal love and joy that transcends all limitations.

KAVINDRA

5

Other books by Jeffrey Armstrong

Karma: The Ancient Science of Cause and Effect
The Vedic Astrology Deck
God/Goddess the Astrologer
The Binary Bible of St. Silicon
Dreaming the Countless Worlds
Swept Away - Volume 1
The Secret of Delight - Volume 2
Sandhya the Twilight of Love - Volume 3
Swan of Endless Love
Lotus Eyes Lotus Feet
This Way Never Lies
Smile When You've Had Enough
The Mountain Climbed Me Up
Black Light of the Goddess
Visions From the Fire
Heart of the Night
75 Light Bulb Jokes

Upcoming Books

The Companion Bhagavad-gita
The UltiMate™ Relationship
Love Letters From a Yogi

"The experience of the union of love with God is so intimate, so vital, and so definitive that the mystical poet, as opposed to the so-called religious poet, will never wonder about the existence or non-existence of God, not even as an aesthetic recourse, just as the existence or non-existence of the air one breathes is never questioned." **Fernando Rielo**, Spanish Poet

"Your work is a direct transmission of transcendental energy...You are the new Rumi."
Patrick Bernard, Award winning producer and composer of devotional music.

"In my opinion Jeffrey Armstrong "Kavindra" is the best living poet in the English language today, a true master among all other English masters. He is an adept at any aspect of poetry whether humor, satire, romance, or what have you. It has been a great honor for me to have been able to follow his poetic evolution for almost three decades now. His poetry is a continuous source of inspiration. Truly peerless!"
Kerry Lawrence Smith, Director of English, Oasis Secondary School, Manaus Amazonas, Brazil

"As I read the poetic verses in *The Night We First Met,* I felt once again that joyful, blissful glimpse of divine love that I had first experienced many years ago when I read Gitanjali of Sri Rabindra Nath Tagore, who was awarded a Nobel prize in literature for his work. I am thrilled to see the depth of experience of Hindu divinity in the verses composed by a nava-Hindu, Sri Kavindra." **Ved Prakash Chaudhary, Ph.D.**
General Secretary, Hindu Collective Initiative (HCI) North America

"You have a God-given gift of words which makes the mystical easy to reach... Upanishadic phrases and beautiful imagery are woven seamlessly with modem symbols. Kavindra has done a service to the English speaking world by bringing out this volume."
Abhinav Dwivedi, Vice President, Hindu University of America, Orlando, Florida

Table of Contents

Table of Contents

Preface
My Wretched Flower

When I was young and heard of Your ancient temple,
Built in a far-off land oriental,

Though I did not know the path, I started walking,
Asking directions from anyone who was talking.

I crossed oceans enraged by typhoons,
I fought mindless wars in nameless platoons.

Though born to be cannon-fodder, I somehow survived,
I was the morsel of which, Death was deprived.

In strange lands I strayed and forgot my quest,
Enraptured by maidens, my mind with drugs obsessed.

I almost stayed in that illusory oasis,
In perfumed tents with the fragrance of Isis

But climbing the mountains, I sought the rugged crags,
Seeking there to escape from human plagues

And in those mighty towers of granite sat,
Trying to remember the original question that

Arose within me prior to my birth,
The quest to find a treasure of great worth.

Then sunrise rose inside me and rent the veil,
Again I remembered Your temple and saw the trail.

Then finally, I spied in the distance Your holy tower,
So, I searched the fields to find an offering flower

But alas, a cactus bloom was all I had,
Brown, covered with thorns and smelling bad.

I carried it to Your altar and placed it there,
Ashamed that my offering could not be something fair.

Bowing to the floor and crying out to You,
Sorry to bring a gift of such deathly hue.

Then suddenly a sweet odour filled the room,
Something was transforming that wretched bloom

And as my eyes opened I saw the wondrous,
My wretched flower had become a fragrant lotus.

Introduction
Guided By Grace

I built my wings
Out of wax and things,
With feathers from falcons and hawks,
Sewn together with thread
From books I had read,
A collection of ancient talks

On the subject of flying
Past the reach of dying,
Spoken by masters of flight.
I trusted their words
To become like the birds
And fly toward the source of the light.

So high on a peak
I had climbed for a week,
I perched on the edge of a wall,
Above an abyss,
Indescribable bliss,
I leapt and started my fall.

Then the wind with a sigh,
Lifted me high,
Higher and higher I glided,
In a spiral ascent
Of enlightenment,
By invisible fingers guided

On inscrutable trails,
With my amateur sails,
Like a ship of faith on the sea,
In the vastness of space,
Yet guided by grace,
I flew toward eternity.

Next I dove in the Sun
Where the truth is all one,
Which burned every trace of my past,
I emerged in the dark,
In the form of a lark,
On a tree growing twisted and vast,

As the Moon rose above
Shining sweetness and love,
So I flew once again to its light.
That nectarian globe
Shed Her silvery robe,
Standing naked alone in the night.

Then She lifted Her hand
As a place I could land
And I dove toward Her shimmering breast,
On the Mother of all
I ended my fall,
In Her heart I now have a nest.

GANAPATI

The elephants dance in a forest
Where once I chanced to go
But you must get past the tigers,
Before you see their show.

Trunks a toss, the tusking gleam
Glints upon their dim eyes bright,
No footprints in the morning,
Where you might have been at night.

And hidden beneath, the wary hare
Awaits the cooling lunar heat,
Peeking out from time to time,
Beneath the dancing thunder feet.

Where the slow-eyed pythons hang like ice,
With flicking tongue, ungrateful worms,
Like languorous convoluted vines
Above the swaying pachyderms.

The locust priests begin their song,
Primeval rhythms, ancient chants,
Invoking gods to golden seats,
Upon the backs of elephants.

Now rearing up the mighty beasts
Pay homage in a swaying line,
Then kneel and raise a joyful cry,
In ecstasy of love divine.

And in a flash their secret comes,
The truth displayed in limbs and parts,
Is just a hint or clue at best,
Of the world within their hearts.

I AM THE VINA THAT SHE PLAYED

I am flying through the endless night,
Without a sound, faster than light,

Migrating toward eternity
The swan of sound that carries me,

Soars above the reach of death,
Upon the silent wind of breath.

Perched upon that subtle wing,
I chart a course past everything.

Up the transverse slopes of time,
Past the peaks you cannot climb,

Beyond the air, beyond the sky,
Past ancient ones who cannot die.

Beyond the edge, with no directions,
Within the center, no reflections,

To where no mind can ever go,
Past the Sun, without a shadow

And on that swan embracing me,
The graceful goddess Sarasvati,

With smiling face, absorbed, intent,
She plays her stringed instrument.

Upon her lap I rest in bliss,
In ecstasy, her song is this

That cannot die and will not fade,
I am the vina that she played.

DIVINE GRACE

With your perfect vision you opened my eyes
And touched my sleeping soul
In its hidden place,
With your loving grace,
I was broken, but you made me whole.

Just when the clouds were filling the skies
And keeping me from the light
I was fading away,
With nothing to say
But you came and restored my sight.

Like the full Moon shining bright on the rise,
You appeared in the sky of my heart
O the heavens rejoice,
At the sound of your voice
And all ignorance has to depart.

Dear master, your words of wisdom so wise,
Have been sent by the Lord from above
To enlighten all men
And teach them again,
The ways of eternal love.

BRIGHT HIGH FLIGHT

Eternal master lead us through the night,
Your footprints in the sky,
Will never die
Or vanish from our sight.

We follow you as soaring eagles fly
Above the mountains' height,
We seek the light
Beyond the Sun on high,

Where lies the spirit worlds in splendour bright;
The tears you cry,
Our broken hearts unite
And sailing in the mercy ship you ply,

We fight the only fight,
For what is right
And change our darkened souls
From black to white.

RAIN OF MERCY

Just as a thunder cloud pours rain
Upon the forests burning plain,

So you your rain of mercy send
Upon devotee flowers who bend

And gently sway upon a breeze,
Their fragrance offered at your knees.

The breeze is soft and gently sighs
The Holy Name beneath summer skies,

Reflections of your loveliness
Upon their budding consciousness.

While black bees humming gather around
To taste the nectar of the sound

You speak, the silver moonbeams dance
And fall beneath your loving glance.

O Prabupada wandering free
Through Vraja's fields in ecstasy,

Please place your feet upon my mind
O lead me father I am blind

But when I hear your soothing voice
I feel my burning heart rejoice.

Lyrics for *Rain of Mercy* on the *Take Me Back* CD produced by Michael Cassidy

KRISHNA SUN

Shadows dance before my eyes they
Touch me in the light of half-day,

Teasing me with sweet distraction
Formed of light's sublime refraction.

Whispering secret innuendo
Dazzling colors like a rainbow,

In the sky of my desire
Kindle in my mind a fire.

Maya calls me to her chamber
It's her duty who can blame her.

Prabupad I hold your feet so
Though I see her I will not go

And I watch the pale horizon
Straining to the east with eyes on

Rosy hues of dawn's arrival,
Birds of love the day's approach call,

Cries my heart: "I hear Him coming!"
Dancing smiling flute song humming.

O Lord I am a morning flower
In Your servant's window bower,

He has grown me for Your pleasure
Planted in my heart a treasure

And You as the Sun are rising
All the darkened world surprising:

Hare Krishna Hare Krishna
Krishna Krishna Hare Hare
Hare Rama Hare Rama
Rama Rama Hare Hare.

GURU VANI

Some people say you have gone away
But your words will never disappear
And so to me through what you say
You live in my heart as long as I hear.

Each morning I clean your sitting place
Then water the seeds you came to plant,
Within my breast your loving grace
Grows daily as I try to chant.

And the Holy Name, your matchless gift,
Deity upon my simple altar,
A stumbling child, I feel you lift
Me gently up, each time I falter.

Gone away in flesh they say
But younger by the day to me,
Who guides me as I find the way?
Or smiles and shares his ecstasy?

Yes, gone for those who think you went
But here to all who daily listen,
To your message, heaven sent,
Within their minds you smile and glisten.

So live forever Jagat Guru
Within the hearts of one and all,
You teach the ways of serving God
And loving your dark-eyed Lord Gopal.

SURRENDER TO LOVE

When first I proposed to be of service,
It was the people who made me nervous

But the unpredictable human being,
Is the one in need of freeing,

In the darkness of matter mired,
So, just as I had been inspired,

I took the vow to wear their yoke,
Could not defend myself by joke

Or distance from their machinations,
The politics that trouble nations.

And no one is ever more the fool,
Than those, who erring, hope to rule.

So, bowing I chose to take a chance,
Trusting the truth and inner guidance,

Flying alone with eternal light,
Holding Their grace night after night,

Pouring the water of wisdom for free,
Crying for them in my ecstasy,

They stripped me naked and ate my heart,
Feasting upon my every part.

Yet there at the moment I had feared,
A miracle of love appeared,

Their hands reached out with tender love,
Around, below, within, above,

I felt their wishes lift me up,
I felt their wonder fill my cup.

I saw within their loving eyes,
The visions of endless paradise,

That had been given once to me,
They bathed me in their ecstasy,

Fed me with their food divine,
Intoxicated on their wine,

I learned to trust and then to surrender,
For they are the Lords to whom I render

The service I first had only held,
Had in the hearts of people swelled.

And thus my trust was well repaid,
By all the people with whom I played.

I poured my nectar into their bowl
And they taught me the final goal,

To be consumed by giving all,
Surrender to love, you will not fall.

ECHO OF THE CONCH

Speak the message of the spirit,
Freedom loving souls will hear it,
A sound that holy wars will launch,
The echo of Lord Krishna's conch.

Through the ether, down the ages
Sung by pure and holy sages,
Received by lost unhappy men,
A battle cry will rise again.

The banner raised within their heart,
Each person will pray to do their part
To serve the Lord with all their might,
To learn what's good and seek the light.

Defeating anger, greed and lust,
A government of love and trust,
Where people strive for higher goals,
Will rule a group of gentle souls,

Who serve the Lord in ecstasy
Without reward eternally,
Unbending souls whose vows are staunch,
Will hear the echo of the conch.

DARK AGE

A veil of evil hangs above the Earth,
Harbinger of night with weapons sharp,
The clarion of doom has taken birth
And crushing love, has broken heaven's harp.

Cement and steel where once the land was green
And clouds of poison fill the threatening sky,
Where rain once fell and rainbows could be seen
The wells and hearts of men will soon be dry.

The clamour of machines has killed the birds,
Who used to fill the morning with their song
And cruel men speak clever sounding words
To secretly confuse the right with wrong.

The rivers, fields and mountains of our lands
A birthright to our children from the Lord,
Have fallen into crooked leaders' hands
And no man dares to lift the sacred sword.

But listen friends, as darkness gathers around,
One light still shines a pure and radiant flame,
Just breaking forth like sunrise is the sound
Of God, Who's come to save us through His name:

Hare Krishna Hare Krishna
Krishna Krishna Hare Hare
Hare Rama Hare Rama
Rama Rama Hare Hare.

21

LAST JOURNEY

Wander weary pilgrim,
Through the deserts of uncertainty,
Past unreasonable mountains
To the shores of unfathomable seas.

Remember this
When the burning winds of desire
Wear at your face,
Chiselling hard lines of anger and frustration,
Where smiles once played.

The scorching sun of eternal time,
Will parch the very life from your blood
And yet you must go on.

Remember you are eternal spirit!
Release your mind
From the stranglehold of past pain
And beware the subtle enchantress
Of vain future hopes.

Real hope based on truth,
Is the precious water you carry,
Use it carefully and guard it well
From the dangerous enemy forgetfulness.
This dread journey
Cannot be stopped halfway.

LAST JOURNEY CONT'D

You must now find the strength to go on,
When all have perished or turned aside.
When night closes in,
And its eerie chill and dark spell
Are all around you.

When all is lost and nothing is left
For comfort or shelter,
Then turn your burning eyes
To the smiling face of the Lord.

He was just waiting for you to see
That the true path
Is within your own heart.

Now you are on your way home,
You no longer care or worry,
Once again you are His,
You have won the gift
No one can take away,
Eternal love.

RESCUING HAND

O small that I am and humbled
By the slavery of anger and lust,
I walked on my own, Lord, but stumbled
And come to You now with my trust.

In a land filled with rivers of tears,
I passed my childhood and youth
Trying to live with my fears
But I come to You now for the truth.

Deluded by flickering pleasure,
I was lashed by the whips cold and hot
And all of my searches for treasure
Turned out to be that which is not.

This bondage to matter is endless,
Like children who play in the sand
We stand on the seashore defenseless,
Except for Your rescuing hand.

A SIGN OF SURRENDER

O cold mechanic desert life
I'm not your child you're not my wife,
Nor will I wear your dusty clothes
I feel the thorn, I've smelt the rose.

Outworn my shoes are growing thin
From trackless miles of wandering sin,
In lands where only cactus grows,
I feel the thorn, I've smelt the rose.

O long the night, and short the day
How cruel December, fragrant May
Was always short and filled with foes,
I feel the thorn, I've smelt the rose.

On Himalayan silent peaks
I sat for years and months and weeks,
Retreating from your painful blows,
I feel the thorn, I've smelt the rose.

So many times the Moon rose high,
And filled with light the darkened sky
Yet I my foolish eyes would close,
I feel the thorn, I've smelt the rose.

And every time the dawn appeared
Its light revealed that which I feared,
A land of death besieged with woes,
I feel the thorn, I've smelt the rose.

The mighty ocean rolls and swells,
Its depths enclose our private hells
But no one all the secrets knows,
I feel the thorn, I've smelt the rose.

Now finally Lord I hear Your song
I'll see You soon, it won't take long
No more Your love will I oppose,
I feel the thorn, I've smelt the rose.

So let my every word and deed
Be free of anger, lust and greed,
For each soul's heart their action shows
I feel the thorn, I've smelt the rose.

O let my chanting fill the skies
So love for You may fill my eyes,
Let serving You be my repose
I feel the thorn, I've smelt the rose.

Lyrics for *Sign of Surrender* on the
Nature's Secret CD produced by Michael Cassidy

LOST AT SEA

I pray, O Lord, my heart is Yours
While traveling near lonely shores,

Where monsters wait and dragons sleep
And dreams of wickedness are deep.

Within the night the tossing waves
Pound the moaning buried graves

Of lost and crying souls, my Lord
This ocean is so deep to ford.

And howling winds, the snake of time,
Has captured me as waters climb

In crushing peaks above my head,
My mind is weak, my body dead.

My soul is wandering in the night,
When suddenly I see a light,

A beam beneath the thundering clouds
That drape the dreadful sky like shrouds.

Above the rushing foamy strand,
I see a rock in splendor stand

And anchored firmly at its height,
A lighthouse with its beacon bright

But like no light I've ever seen,
It glows so radiant and serene,

Amidst the terrors of the dark
And guides my torn and battered bark.

That light then cuts a lucent swath,
Through ignorance so black, a path

Bright hope shines forth amid the reefs,
Of hate and endless bleak beliefs.

LOST AT SEA CONT'D

But Lord, is this some conjurer's trick?
How can light stand in dark so thick?

Or have You finally sent Your grace,
To save me from this hopeless place?

I pray, O Lord, my heart is true,
That I may someday come to You

And reach the distant ocean's shore,
To live with You forevermore.

I pray O Lord, my heart is Yours,
While traveling near distant shores.

WINK AT DEATH

Like a tiger stalking the deer,
You will not know when Death is near.

There is no system of early warning,
No memo on your desk that morning,

No time to put your affairs in order,
No way back from across that border,

For when the cosmic mind is made,
The appointment cannot be delayed.

There are too many souls to reap,
There is no object you can keep

And though it seems to be from here,
Death is not something we should fear,

No more than you fear changing clothes,
Nor can forever keep a rose.

There is no posture or position,
From which to avoid that transition.

So do it now, embrace your death,
Release your stranglehold on breath.

Raise your hands up to the sky
And shout that you will never die.

Look the Reaper in the face,
And welcome Him with joy and grace.

Like a dancer, run and leap,
Shedding what you cannot keep.

Prepare to take that final trip,
Take off your body like a strip,

Dancing upon this worldly stage,
As if your passing is all the rage.

Wink at Death and flirt with Demise,
Fly beyond to paradise.

Death is not under your control
But only you can be the soul.

SECOND BIRTH

When dawn shook the stars with her bursting ray,
As burgeoning life shoots forth from earthly clay,

Night, rent asunder, split and fell from sight,
Banished by the rosy steeds of Helios' light.

This moment the soul is reborn and lives to die,
Second-birth, blessed moment, of breaking the tie

That binds the spirit to Earth, the sharpened sword,
Cuts illusions nets and slays the savage horde

Of demons, the doubts that darkened the soul
With chaos and turned her away from the goal.

Day blossoms, the lotus of youth faces east
And drinks the golden nectar of hope, a feast

In honor of truth, is announced to the few,
Who hunger and thirst on the path of the true

Living light, streaming down from the beautiful face,
Of God, out of sight and beyond outer space.

Hear the music celestial announcing Their glory,
Heralding the arrival of Their holy story,

O life, you were made in Their glorious image,
Go on in your journey with new strength and courage,

29

SECOND BIRTH CONT'D

For life leads you homeward, if only you will,
Hear the sweet voice within you so soft and so still,

Singing all through the night, until the coming of dawn,
Of Their love in your heart, then when darkness is gone,

You will see Them and touch Them and fall at Their feet
And then you will know that your life is complete.

DEFEAT OF SPRING

As Springtime danced across the mountains' shining golden peaks,
She dressed the hills in purple flowers from her blushing cheeks

And kissed the breeze beneath the trees with lips of southern flame
But even she could not outshine my passion for the Holy Name.

Her beauty, beauty still, but somehow different than before,
Like a little pool of water on the mighty ocean shore

Or like the drops of water in the hoof print of a cow,
Were not enough to tempt me from my sacred chanting vow.

For who once tasting nectar will accept the bitter draught?
And who while wandering free would not be sorry to get caught?

The clever serpent wears a rainbow jewel upon his head
And smiling waits in darkness with unblinking eyes of red.

But feeling once Your lotus flower how can one forget?
Nor having once received Your mercy ever pay the debt.

O Shyamasundar cowherd boy, far lovelier than May,
You simply smiled and called my name and stole my love away.

IN A BHAGAVAD-GITA

In a gada de vida,
Krishna spoke the Bhagavad-gita.

Arjuna's slumber was so deep,
He feared the fruit the war would reap.

And Yudhisthira, Dharma's child,
Spoke softly there amid the wild,

While Bhima broke the evil back
Of Duryodhana's eternal lack.

There heroes waving endless flags,
Fought the fight that finally drags

The foe to face the cosmic judge,
Some fought for truth and some for grudge.

There in their midst the Lord of all,
Destined each to rise and fall.

Chess Master on the board of life,
Moved each piece amid the strife

And played the game in stepwise motion,
Rivers of blood, the endless ocean,

Rose and fell within their veins,
On elephants' backs and horses' manes,

They rode the epic truth to bare,
While love and honor glistened there.

And listening to the Eternal Lord,
Arjuna wielded bow and sword.

He stood amidst the angry foe,
Upon the chariot, fast or slow,

He fought but did not do a thing,
Straining to hear Lord Krishna sing,

He stood, the soul upon that field,
Driven by the Lord to yield,

He raced triumphant to the goal,
Surrender wins the warring soul.

A CHANGE OF HEART

The caterpillar changed his mind
And woke to find himself refined,

His old self had to die
For him to be a butterfly.

He tired of walking on the ground
And so around himself he wound,

A screen of silken strands,
A veil untouched by human hands.

Then something subtle changed within,
Reflected by his changing skin,

He had a change of heart
And wished to play another part.

If like that worm my soul can fly
A rainbow colored butterfly,

Upon the winds of time
Then I with wings of gold will climb

Beyond this burning dark abyss
Up to that land of love and bliss,

Where grows a flower sweet,
I'll fly to Krishna's lotus feet

And there I'll live eternally,
My soul at last from matter free

A song will fill the sky.
The love song of a butterfly.

Lyrics for *Change of Heart* on the
Change of Heart CD produced by Michael Cassidy

I SAW THE LIGHT

I saw the light
Coming down from the face,
Of the beautiful Lord
Far beyond outer space.

So radiant and bright
Shining perfectly clear,
Descending in glory
And removing all fear.

Once in the night
I did wander in pain,
Praying for sunrise,
To see Him again.

Then from great height
Came a vision of grace,
Pure causeless mercy,
From a transcendent place.

Well I know it is right
When I see Him so near,
In the sky of my heart
In my eye as a tear.

O grant me my sight,
Let me stand in the rain,
Of Your rainbow of love,
The eternal refrain:

Om namo bhagavate vasudevaya

Lyrics for *There is a Light* on the
Beyond Illusion CD produced by Michael Cassidy

THE ENDLESS BATTLE

Like an advancing army, survival has marched upon my soul,
Taking the high ground in a struggle raging out of control.

Machines of war, smoke and flames, poisons fill the air,
Doubts like demons drag me down into their stinking lair

Relentless darkness covers me, the fog of night and sleep,
Illusions taunt my hungry heart with dreams I cannot keep.

Three fierce generals raise their banners above the swirling dust,
Endless columns trudge behind them: anger, greed and lust

Attack with crushing battle cries, the hearts of all who hear,
The piercing sound of matter grinding down the human sphere.

While I ride in my chariot, a shining golden car,
Pulled by five white milky steeds, my flag the Northern Star.

Across the sacred field of action, racing into the fray,
Releasing arrows all around, to drive the dark away

And while I fight my Unseen Driver dodges right and left,
Placing my life in unknown hands, driven with motions deft,

I stand upon my pounding heart, fighting to be free,
With spears of justice, swords of love and arrows of honesty.

The battle rages across the ages without a sign of peace,
Until we stand in another land, having finally found release.

So stay on the battlefield protected by the shield of truth and light
And trust the Invisible Driver to lead you beyond the land of night.

DEATH IS OUR BEST FRIEND

It is possible that Death is our best friend,
A giant come to play and not the end.

It is possible that Death is a transit on a train,
A moment of confusion and then no pain.

It could be Death is just our next promotion,
Jumping from the puddle to an ocean.

It may be that Death is highly over-rated,
That Life continues even more integrated.

It might be fear itself instead of Death,
That is the very nature of each breath.

Perhaps life itself is the source of fear
And Death is going home to all that's dear.

Imagine we've had it backwards all this time,
That Life is a valley and Death a mountain climb.

What if Life is a river and Death the shore,
Where friends wait to play with us once more.

It could be that Life is a class and Death the exam
And the subject is finally knowing who I am.

Or perhaps Life is a chess game we just won
And Death is the sign the next one has begun.

Death could be a telegram from bliss,
A cosmic orgasm or intergalactic kiss.

It may be that Death is the prelude to a dance,
Where all the stars in the sky are the audience.

Then what if Death is God's dinner bell,
The call to a feast where everyone eats like hell.

And Heaven is a party that never quits,
Where everyone gets the Prince and the slipper fits.

Perhaps the part of Death that we resist,
Is doubting we are on the party list.

It might be we have forgotten we are love,
Just like that which waits for us above.

It wouldn't surprise me that we have become confused,
Thinking that Death is Life being abused.

Perhaps we forgot that Death is married to Life,
That we are
            their children
                and They
                    are husband
                        and wife!

WHY THE SKY IS BLUE

Upon the lotus in Vishnu's navel,
The universe began to unravel,

There Brahma sat with Sarasvati,
Her mantra gave him Shakti-pati,

So once upon a time began,
Which led to woman and her man.

The waters rolled, the darkness split,
Light arose, the Devas grasped it

And darkness, home of death and sin,
Fell from Brahma like a skin,

The Asuras grabbed it with a cry
And thus the lovers of dark must die.

Then one by one each thing arose,
Brought forth in ways that no one knows.

As Shiva awoke from endless trance,
Played his drum and began to dance,

Shooting sparks in all directions,
Gushing fire from His erections,

With Shakti wrapped in mad orgasm,
They wove the webs of ectoplasm,

Spun the sheaths and made the web,
Awakened the souls who had been dead,

While great tsunamis from the ocean,
Began to spin with a spiral motion.

The seven planets singing notes,
Orchestrated the floating motes,

Into patterns reverberating,
Octaves up and down gyrating,

Songs emerged, a cosmic choir,
One by one crawled from the mire,

Singing out in every key,
The myriad species ranging free,

Swam and ran and flew through space,
Finding homes in every place.

Then Vishnu set the motions right,
While Lakshmi bathed them in Her light.

Clouds rolled back, the Sun appeared,
Driving away the doubt and fear.

A honey Moon with nectar sweet,
Poured life into the food we eat

WHY THE SKY IS BLUE CONT'D

And air in gentle vespers played,
Across this endless world remade,

The cosmic lotus bloomed and grew
And that is why the sky is blue.

STAND AWAKE

Just as water conforms to its container,
So consciousness appears to its maintainer.

I am was there before I am was dressed
In cloaks of matter, covered and repressed.

The state of purest being was never meant,
To become the material covering nature lent

But was allowed to ride within that car,
To learn of itself as an eternal star,

To taste the infinite shapes and forms of bliss,
To study: "thou art that," in the midst of this,

To taste the delicious flavours as lad or lassie,
While always remembering our nature:
"Aham Brahmasmi."

But if we call our conscious self the veil,
Our higher self is lost and bound to fail.

Eternal knower, purusha, person divine,
Sent to the realms of matter to learn the design.

The unconscious covering is just the net,
In a game whose purpose every soul must get.

So stand on the chariot wielding the bow of mind
And fire the arrows of truth until the blind

Rulers of this slumbering world awake,
Blow the conch of consciousness until they shake.

Stand awake and never accept defeat,
Flying the flag of Krishna's lotus feet.

THE GOLDEN AVATAR

In India five hundred years ago,
The Lord of all from out of boundless grace
Appeared His causeless mercy to bestow,
Upon a blind and suffering human race.

He came to save the lost souls from disgrace,
Appearing as the sages had foretold,
A gentle loving smile upon His face
And shining with the hue of purest gold.

Descending on this planet filled with woe,
A lonely island lost in outer space,
He sang and love of God began to flow
Like crystal water from a silver vase.

The rising Moon was veiled in shadow lace,
A silken starlight mantle did enfold
The birth of He no darkness could erase
And shining with the hue of purest gold.

The winter night was filled with His sweet glow,
His lotus-flower, conch-shell, disk and mace
The power of the Holy Name would show,
The darkness of this winter age untrace

And even benedict the low and base,
From neither man nor beast will He withhold.
His love will fill their hearts and hate replace
And shining with the hue of purest gold.

Gauranga's brought His love to this dark place,
Just hear Him chanting, dance and sing, behold
The Holy Name within His heart's embrace
And shining with the hue of purest gold.

SANKIRTAN

White clouds of mercy overhung
My mind, like lowing herds
Of ancient kine and there among
Were whispered fairest words.

Beyond the dust of golden hooves,
A song rang out sublime,
So off I ran as it behooves
But fools to stay in time,

Which straight away shot past my ear,
Toc-ticking all the while
And in the distance I could hear
A tune that made me smile.

The stars were dancing on the wind,
A chorus filled the sky,
With drums that ghinned and boomed and dhinned;
Sweet cymbals bright and high.

Above the clouds a kirtan roared
And swung in ecstasy,
Devotees laughing, danced and soared
In praise of Lord Hari.

Up and down, with a swaying motion,
Shouting Hari bol!
Like sharks within a nectar ocean,
In transports of the soul.

Decorated with spiritual gems,
Divine enraptured signs,
Like shining emerald diadems,
Like drunkards, on the best of wines,

Perspiring, laughing, shaking, trembling,
Like soaring birds of prey,
From every far-off place assembling,
Their numbers swell and sway.

Then from their midst a form of gold
Leaps madly into space
And all in wondrous awe behold,
The Lord's transcendent grace.

Shri Chaitanya, O Gauranga,
Tears in vast profusion,
Groups with kartal and mridanga,
Wildness and confusion,

41

SANKIRTAN CONT'D

Rushing through the universe
In search of Krishna's feet,
Govinda das recites a verse,
The drum picks up the beat,

Too late! The damage now is done,
Sweet showers from above,
Descend to Earth, on everyone,
A rain of purest love,

Chaitanya's mercy floods the ground,
On men and beasts and trees
And up they fly with a humming sound,
Like a frenzied swarm of bees.

Then off across the sky, like geese
Migrating to fairer places,
With smiles of delight at their sweet release,
Shining from their faces.

WHITE ISLAND

There is a distant place called Svetadvip,
Where lying down in silent cosmic sleep,
Surrounded by a milky ocean white,
Within a castle on an island bright,

The Universal Lord, sweet smiling, dreams
And from His moon-like face soft lucent beams
Shine forth revealing gold and silver halls,
Green emeralds, rubies, carven ivory walls

Where endless rows of pillars formed of pearl,
Are swept by towering ocean waves that curl
And toss their foamy nectar all through space.
Gold earrings decorate His smiling face,

A flower garland rests upon His chest,
In silken yellow garments He is dressed,
With blackish hair that curls about His ears,
His lotus-petal eyes remove all fears.

Complexion blackish like a thunder cloud,
His graceful form with four strong arms endowed,
Is resting on a soft white serpent bed,
With pointed tongues and fearsome eyes of red,

A thousand headed snake with bluish scales
Is coiling far beyond this world of veils
And lying there Narayan casts His glance
Across the endless miles of ignorance.

He enters in the heart of all that be,
Each golden sunbeam shows His majesty,
His Holy Name is filled with nectar sweet
And purest love flows from His lotus feet.

Lyrics for *Swetadwip* on the *Change of Heart* CD
produced by Michael Cassidy

ARE'TIST

O have you heard the laughter
Play beneath the ancient bows,
Of silver trees with hair of gold
Where lovers made their vows

Or watched the clouds down pouring
And felt that raindrops all are tears,
Have you ever lived a moment
For a hundred thousand years?

Then perhaps you've seen a sunrise
Shining like a brilliant eye
Or felt the Moon embracing you
From high up in the sky.

You might have even noticed
The dewdrop diamonds on the green,
If you've been watching carefully
All this you must have seen.

And if you never blinked
You must have seen the Artist's hand,
Painting slowly with His brush
Upon the canvas land.

OUT OF THE BLUE

Listen to the music of the morning,
The gentle voices whispering in the night,
Among the trees,
The humming bees,
Are singing songs of harmony and light.

Ocean waves are pounding out a rhythm,
The Moon conducts a symphony sublime,
The stars that shine,
Each sing a line
And all the planets dance to keep in time.

Mountains sit in silent meditation,
The faces in the clouds go floating by
And drops of rain,
A cool refrain,
Teach everyone the art of how to cry.

Sunshine touches all of us with kindness,
The rainbows arching softly in the blue
And winging birds,
Like subtle words,
Each part of nature offers us a clue.

Laughter rolls throughout the sky like thunder,
The wise ones bow their heads, and smiling nod,
For nature's grace,
Reflects the face
And all the wondrous beauty that is God.

Listen to the music of the morning,
The gentle voices whispering in the night,
Among the trees,
The humming bees,
Are singing songs of harmony and light.

YOU TAUGHT THE BIRDS TO SING

You taught the birds to sing
Songs they could never have known,
Acrobats of feather and wing,
Writing messages where they have flown.

You sat among the trees,
Teaching under their waving leaves,
A feathered choir, such melodies,
To the pipe organ summer breeze.

You composed an ode to love,
Beneath the autumn rains,
With winged acolytes above,
Chirping their glad refrains.

You wrote notes with ink and quills
On parchments that will never die
And trained the angels yellow bills,
To sing them while they fly.

You taught the birds to sing of us,
Songs about the love we share,
A concert sweet and wondrous,
Now written on the air.

WITHIN THE WIND

Reaching out from within the wind
I feel Your fingertips,
Mixed in an intoxicating blend.
I taste Your lips,

With my mouth upon a peach,
I smell Your scent.
You are almost in my reach,
In every subtle hint.

Burning deep within the fire,
I feel Your need.
Each note of music is Your desire,
Planted like a seed.

Upon a full Moon night, my mind
Sees Your light within,
In everything You are entwined
Like a fragrance on the wind.

ONE NIGHT I STOLE ALL YOUR BEAUTY

One night I circled the globe,
While everyone else slept,
I stole all Your beauty
And hid it beneath my robe.

In a silver locket, on a chain,
With a gold clasp on the side,
All Your glory lay concealed upon my heart,
While the rest of the world went insane.

They searched everywhere and cried,
Desperate to gaze upon Your sweetness,
Starving for a taste of Your divinity.
When they knocked upon my door I lied:

No, there is none of Krishna's beauty here,
I said, like you I am wasting away.
Then, laughing, I entered my closet
And sat all night gazing at You my dear.

Finally, their cries became so loud,
I invited them all to my house,
Served cookies, tea and jam
And chastised them for being so proud.

I'm going to give the Beauty back
But first you must apologize
To the poor, the sick, the gentle and wise,
To everyone whose light you turned to black.

ONE NIGHT I STOLE ALL YOUR BEAUTY CONT'D

If Beauty returns, you must promise me this,
That every step you take each day,
Will serve the cause of Beauty's way.
They agreed, and Beauty turned to bliss.

Then You stepped from the locket and hugged each one,
Kissed their lips and set them spinning,
Danced with them all evening
And filled the darkness with them like the Sun.

ALL THAT EXISTS IS WITHIN

All that exists is within
And repeated without once again.

What is above is below,
The tree in the seed that will grow.

The world has nothing outside
But that which, within we hide

And each is equally free
To turn inside and see.

Unlimited realms to explore,
A staircase that leads to a door,

A lock with a skeleton key,
A window that looks on the sea,

A ship set to sail at the dawn,
A journey that goes on and on.

The mystical isle of our dreams,
Appearing without, so it seems

But shining eternally free,
In realms meant for ecstasy,

It waits on a distant shore,
The journey we're longing for,

Begins on trails in our heart
And ends where we first had our start.

IF THE BIRDS SANG ALL AT ONCE

If the birds all sang at once,
To the glorious rising of Your golden eye
And each sunbeam became a different note,
Until their symphony filled the entire sky.

If the full Moon raced madly
Across the firmament to kiss each star,
Then fell exhausted on a mountain peak
And they turned themselves into a celestial car.

If dewdrops became seeds of bliss
And the wind blew them across the Earth,
Where they grew to fragrant trees
Giving joy and love another birth.

If every loving thought took flight,
A butterfly with iridescent wings
And they were free but let themselves be caught
So Your love would land on human beings.

Then Sun, stars, Moon and dew,
Would race singing love birds across the sky,
Amidst a forest of loving fruit
And You and I would be a butterfly.

I SEE YOUR BEAUTY

I see Your beauty in all directions,
Exquisite glory in splendiferous profusion,
Tumbling down in rivulets of mad confusion
Infinite points of luminous divine projection

Ripple and cascade in concert,
Spiral and spin in fractal galactic forms
Clash and collide in flashing cosmic storms,
Splash in a raging flood across a desert

Painting a wild proliferation,
Blooming tangled flower paths of glory,
Clinging to the face of granite mountains hoary,
Driving birds to warble their ecstatic orchestration.

Thunder and lightning, a billion eyes,
Screaming a wild cry, lovers kiss,
Neighing horses stampede across a cliff,
Night explodes into blinding star skies.

O my Lord, You are a glorious
Goddess, gorgeous, inconceivable effigy,
Reflected on the uncountable mirrors of eternity
Sung by endless hymns and instruments uproarious.

I see beauty everywhere,
Beauty, beauty, mindless truth insane,
Beyond all knowing yet displayed again and again,
Everywhere I look, I see Your beauty there.

COULD OUR DESIRE FOR JOY BE TRUTH AT LAST

(Bhagavan, the Executive Summary)

Listen friend, for time cannot be trusted,
This life of ours is a puzzle upon a table,
It is a lock whose key has somehow rusted
But we must find the secret while we are able.

First, observe we do not want to die,
We cling to youth and do not wish to age.
The pain of birth causes all to cry
And disease overtakes us at a certain stage.

Notice how we resist the idea of death,
Desire stays fresh until our dying day,
We swim in air, unconscious of our breath,
We're forced to work, yet wish that we could play.

At first we seek the pleasures of this world
And then become an addict to our passion,
Swept by circumstance our life is hurled
Down paths unknown, by politics or fashion.

We work for fools, serve masters with no name,
Go into debt for things we do not need,
Neglect our soul, while chasing gain and fame,
Driven by anger, a prisoner of greed.

COULD OUR DESIRE FOR JOY BE TRUTH AT LAST CONT'D

As children we are impatient to be old,
In youth we burn too hot and waste our breath,
In old age we lament, turn grey, go cold
And spend our savings trying to run from death.

Each animal has a natural habitat,
They mate in season, live their lives and die
But humans have no home, think on that,
We are the only creatures who wonder why.

Building dams and bridges, flying to space,
Eight-lane freeways polluting the planet's air,
We drive and are driven in the endless human race
But in the end, our race is going where?

Is it progress, making our wheels go faster?
Surrounded by strangers with phones, we are alone,
Have we not become the means of our own disaster?
Reaping the seeds of destruction that we have sown.

Seeing all this, some argue we should renounce,
Give up desire and enter the endless void,
In sadness and frustration they denounce
The beauty and pleasure previously enjoyed.

No God, no self, no joy, just emptiness,
An addict in withdrawal, a silent stone,
Annihilation becomes their happiness,
Iconoclastic, they sit in the dark alone.

COULD OUR DESIRE FOR JOY BE TRUTH AT LAST CONT'D

To enter the void and remove the self they chant,
Counting breaths in silence and retreat,
Nirvana, the path of those who live but can't,
Detachment without beauty is defeat.

Ponder this, is the sum of life a zero,
Are beauty, truth and love an empty illusion
Or are we on a quest, an eternal hero,
Trying to wake and find our true conclusion?

Another view that haunts us is the One,
"The drop becomes the ocean," its teachers say,
"Your you will be the all when you are done,
Homogenize! Give up your personal way.

The world is illusion, form is an ancient lie,
Distinctiveness is a web illusion wove,"
But only oneness means that love must die,
For eternal individuals are the ones who love.

"Those who know don't speak," these pundits opine,
"And those who speak don't know," they again repeat,
Not seeing the flaw in their argument's design,
That saying not to speak is their defeat!

Another oneness trick is called the "now,"
As if there was just one from which to choose
But if there was we would already know how
And "oneness" would mean no one could ever lose.

COULD OUR DESIRE FOR JOY BE TRUTH AT LAST CONT'D

And teachers of oneness could not presume to teach,
Unless there was another to teach it to,
Which makes the oneness a thing no one can preach
Without becoming illusioned by the "two."

So think again, is oneness what we seek?
Is merging in an ocean why we tried
To live our joy and reach the mountain's peak?
Is the truth of our uniqueness that God lied?

Then what is left if drowning in the One
Is a trap in which unknowing souls are caught?
And the void is an empty room with joy for none,
If the world is a place of death with danger fraught?

But what if our final choice is a realm of love,
Where souls enjoy throughout eternity,
What if this world is reflected from above,
A photograph of the place we are meant to be?

Could our desire for joy be the truth at last,
Our attraction to beauty the symptom of our soul?
Our nature to live where anxiety is in the past,
Could the pleasures of endless love become our goal?

EKANTIN

Shining bright in every eye, playing gently,
Teasing beams of, laughing lightly,

Hidden faces, winking out the wordless,
Sprightly smiling message, who would guess,

The hidden manifest, an open secret,
Sees, reflected seeing, myriad mirrors it.

Spinning circles, atoms dancing merrily;
Warbling this, the songbird's ecstasy,

Trilling up the high empyrean dome,
Circles of the seventh heaven roam

And search in silence the dauntless night,
The topless depths and bottomless height.

Within the flower petal maze of fragrance,
Drunk with beauty, drunk with but a glance.

Again, the sweetest well out-rushing,
Sweeping sleeping life, with gushing

Beauty hushing in the timeless deeps
And dropping seeps, within each cell it leaps.

But living life, the secret keeps within,
Pretending to be hidden on the skin.

Brightly shines the image day and night,
The hidden Lord, within our seeing, out of sight.

MY RELIGION IS BEAUTY

My religion is beauty,
I have no other deity,
To serve is my only duty,
My lover's lips are piety.

My God is a Goddess,
Embracing a tender youth,
My offering a soft caress,
My passion the highest truth.

My altar is the heart,
A lotus pulsing pink,
Where lives my counterpart,
I feel therefore I think.

My temple is the sky,
A candle bright, the sun,
The rainbow in your eye,
The stars are everyone.

At night my stained glass window
Shines the Moon inside,
Illuminating with its glow
A joy I cannot hide.

The ocean deep is a chalice,
An offering sublime,
My body, a pleasure palace,
The ocean waves are time

And beauty is eternal,
The embodiment of grace,
Forever fresh and vernal,
The Truth's enchanting face.

SOMEONE SENDS ME FLOWERS

Every spring
Someone sends me flowers,
Without a note,
A Secret Admirer
Plies me with bouquets,
Fills my room with fragrance,
Inflames my heart
With sweet perfumes.
At night, warm breezes
Touch me, caress me,
Until I awake aching,
Unable to sleep,
Dreaming of a Stranger,
Whispering in the bushes,
Lilacs nod and murmur,
Bees buzz with insomnia.
A nightingale sits watching
Without a note.
Again I look for signs,
Footprints at the door,
Lead into my heart.
Music in the distance
Wakes me into summer.
Covered with petals,
My bed smells like heaven.
Every spring,
Someone sends me flowers.

GOLOKA VRINDAVANA

Vrindavan is such a wonderful place
Where bumblebees hum and songbirds sing,
While cowherd boys and monkeys race,
Across the hills their voices ring.

And the rushing sound of the waterfalls
Plays in the caves on Govardhan Hill,
Sweetly covering the crickets' calls
While the sounds of musical laughter spill,

Across a green and grassy field,
Filled with white surabhi cows,
While rivers of milk they lovingly yield
And tears flow from their gentle brows.

Where desire trees' boughs touch the ground
In humble devotion, offering their fruit
And praying to hear the blissful sound
Of Shyamasundar's golden flute.

Goloka Goloka my heart's delight
Where colourful peacocks dance in joy
And pretty gopi damsels roam
In search of a blackish cowherd boy.

Goloka Goloka my heart's delight,
Divine loving lotus with fragrance sweet,
Land of the endless full Moon night,
Of searching the woods for His lotus feet.

Oh let me be a speck of dust
Upon the path where He may dance,
To satisfy the milkmaids' lust
With nectar from His restless glance.

THE LIMBS OF YOGA

Drop your defences,
Pull back your senses,
Withdrawing them in like a turtle,
Move from sensation
To imagination,
The external is yoga's first hurdle.

Do not eat too little
Or too much, seek the middle,
Ignoring both pleasures and pains,
Your senses are horses,
Their objects the courses
And your mind that controls them, the reins.

Discernment, the driver,
Sensations, a river,
The body a chariot bold,
Where the passenger soul,
Must remember the goal,
A realm that never grows old.

That the mind is the friend
Or enemy will depend
On whether it is broken or whole,
Fragmented or one,
Like night or the Sun,
Serving matter or serving the soul.

With one-pointed focus
And a transcendent locus,
Attachment to matter will wane,
The scars in the heart
Will begin to depart
And thoughts will be clear once again.

When your posture or pose,
Turns to conscious repose,
A balance of knowing and static,
Your breath blends with air,
Moving soft everywhere,
A door opens toward the ecstatic.

In this balanced state,
You enter that gate,
By means of vibrations revealed,
With a mantra, in time,
We approach the sublime,
Our true nature is slowly revealed.

Those sanctified words,
Reveal that two birds
Are perched on a tree in our breast,
One the Witness Supreme,
While the other in dream,
Looks for joy in a material nest.

THE LIMBS OF YOGA CONT'D

But the yogi knows better
Than to burrow in matter,
Where death and decay rule the world,
So the bird starts to fly
Toward a spiritual sky,
As the journey within is unfurled.

Past the layers of matter,
Earth, fire and water,
Past wind and still chanting past space,
Past the sirens of mind,
Past logic that's blind,
To the transcendent that isn't a place.

Now samadhi begins
That great burner of sins,
We become like the goal we have sought,
Meditation is kiss,
Mantra turns into bliss,
We are wrapped now where once we were caught.

Now our future is sealed,
Divine forms are revealed,
Within and beyond all is Om,
On through spiritual gates,
Vishnu celebrates,
Another soul has gone home.

I AM AN ISLAND

I am a small island
Around which a storm is raging,
Snarling waves pound my strand,
Swirling eddies and tides are surging.

Shattered lives and flying debris,
Drowning souls I cannot save,
Float face down in front of me,
Battered by each wave.

Yet I am safe, a sheltered cove
Protects my beach, my fragile shore,
A sky of blue and Sun above,
I chant Your Holy Names once more.

Rama, Krishna, Vishnu, Hari,
Shyamasundar, Shambhu, Gopala,
Sita Devi, Radha, Lakshmi,
Ganesha, Sarasvati, on my mala.

They draw a circle around my isle,
Shining their moon-like rays,
Warming me always with their smiles,
They love me in a million ways.

AUM

Hear of the pleasures held for the soul,
Amorous pastimes in green wooded lands,
Revelling parts of an Infinite Whole,
Ecstatic thrills at the touch of their hands.

The King of Devotion, there with His herds
Roving the hills, with a band of dear friends,
In search of enjoyment, their echoing words
Shine through eternity, sweet music blends.

Happiness growing out wild in the fields,
Never diminished, unlimited light,
Always increasing their roaming yields
Absolute Being with no end in sight.

Under a tree, shining forth glowing beams,
The magic of love, in the land of our dreams.

MAGIC MELODIES

Dulcet notes caress across
Ragged chasm miles,
Kissing down a velvet path,
Embracing distant isles.

Enshrouded mountain mystical,
Moon-glow shining peak,
Nightingales in harmony,
Sound the path to seek.

Descending raindrop symphony,
Played on flower petals,
Echoes far their fragrance,
Crimson on the evening settles.

Graceful swans glide silver rings
Sunset sounds a single note,
A petal falls without a sound,
From lotuses that float.

Again the piping euphony
Up dances through the trees,
Someone in the forest calls
My heart with magic melodies.

CHINTAMANI

Lotus-eyed flute song
If you can sing along,
Takes you to another land
Made of love not sand.

Where a desire tree
Made of chintamani,
Nestles over a jewelled seat
Humming bees and flowers sweet,

Birds of love fly above
Cuckoo soft and white dove.
Radha tastes the mellow bliss
Of Her Lord Govinda's kiss.

Lovely gopis dance and sing,
In the bushes whispering.
Cows and cowherds gather round
Swooning to the lovely sound.

Krishna steals the hearts of all
Who can hear His flute song call,
Dance and sing in ecstasy
In Vrindavan wandering free.

Lotus-eyed flute song
If you can sing along,
Takes you to another land
Made of love not sand.

ACME OF ENTITY

The fountain of youth, beauty and truth
Dressed in garments of yellow silk,
Lives in Vrindavan where rivers of milk
Over-flood the land at the sound of His flute.

The Cause of all causes and primeval Lord,
His smiling face, the king of all Moons,
Eternally sports in lotus lagoons
With nothing to do but dance and sing.

The Master of mystics and source of all
In the form of a blackish cowherd boy,
Plays with His friends in pastimes of joy
And their laughing and joking floods the land.

NAUGHTY BOY DAMODAR

Naughty boy Damodar bound by ropes,
The knot will hold, Your mother hopes
But only You know what You've done,
She loves You more than anyone.

A chubby blue baby with restless eyes
And soft pink feet, caught by surprise,
Naughty boy Damodar bound by ropes
The knot will hold, Your mother hopes.

You stole her butter and ran to play,
Fed the monkeys then hid away
In a lonely spot, with a frightened face
But she found You and then began the race.

Faster and faster Your mother ran after,
Naughty boy, Damodar shaking with laughter,
Finally is caught but the rope is too short
By inches she's missed You, what lovely sport!

Naughty boy Damodar bound by ropes,
The knot will hold, Your mother hopes.
She's got You now, You naughty boy.
So You'll have to stay and give us joy.

With fetters of love she has You tied,
Strengthened by the tears You cried,
For ropes are one day torn apart
But bonds of love are in the heart.

Naughty boy Damodar bound by ropes,
The knot will hold, Your mother hopes
But only You know what you've done,
She loves You more than anyone.

LOOK THIS WAY

O Govinda of unsurpassable splendour,
Bowing my head I turn to You and surrender.
Far from the worldly noise, the lonely confusion,
Past the passing of time and matter's illusion.

O Gopala most kind and radiant Master,
Please hear my song and help me come to You faster.
Holding my heart in my hands I bow down completely,
Now appear in my mind and speak to me sweetly.

O Shri Krishna, with eyes like a lotus flower,
Playing Your flute in the shade of a bamboo bower,
Far from this world of death and endless pain,
Please cast Your glance and give me life again.

GOPINATHA

To what can Govinda's form compare?
The flowers of spring are but His smile
And songbirds in all their finery bear
A hint of His subtle artistic style.

The moon-like glow of His smiling face
Has risen above two pillars called arms;
His middle a cool delightful terrace,
Sweet meeting place of secret charms.

Outside the doorway, inviting chest,
Two elephants stand, their trunks His thighs
And palms like lotus flowers rest
Beneath the starlight of His eyes.

Two hips like dens on summer's eve
Arched brow where Cupid learned to dance,
Soft fingernails like bamboo leaves,
Red lips of smiling elegance.

Embraced by garlands, cheeks a flush,
White pomegranate teeth, ripe fruit,
The gopis' hearts like rivers rush,
Enchanted by His golden flute.

GOVINDAM

I offer my most respectful obeisances unto the Absolute Truth,
Eternally present in His abode in the form of eternal youth.

I worship Govinda, the primeval Lord, the first progenitor who
Is tending cows yielding all desire, His complexion heavenly blue.

Like a blackish cloud, with a peacock feather rainbow on His head
And a flute in His hands, His blooming eyes like lotus petals spread.

In the land of spiritual gems, surrounded by millions of purpose trees
And always served by hundreds and thousands of lakshmis or gopis.

Around His neck swings a garland of flowers, His unique loveliness
Charming millions of Cupids, such splendid beauty does He possess.

I worship Shyamasundar, with the moon-locket on His chest,
Whose graceful three-fold bending form is eternally manifest.

His hands are adorned with the golden flute and jeweled ornaments
And He always revels in pastimes of joy, with His loving confidants.

ANKLE BELLS

Softly tinkling through the vales and dells,
Floats the sound of Krishna's ankle bells,

Mingling with the rush of waterfalls
And the cuckoo sings her morning calls.

Sunbeams spread their fingers through the boughs
Of the ageless trees, that shelter cows,

Calves, and cowherd boys who dance and sing,
Through the Vraja forest wandering.

Brilliant peacocks dance in ecstasy,
Shyamasundar's lotus feet to see.

Dark blue rain clouds fill the amber sky,
Over grasses green, where gopis cry,

Madly searching for a cowherd boy,
Krishna, who has stolen all their joy.

Searching for His footprints on the ground,
Languishing to hear His flute song sound.

THE GOLDEN FLUTE

The flute piped out a single note,
I dropped my load to listen,
That note became a bird and flew
Across my dark horizon.

The bird became a butterfly
That landed very near,
It then became a buzzing bee
And stung me in the ear.

I shrieked, I cried, like one gone mad,
I ran throughout the night
But when I stopped my eyes were blind
And ears were now my sight.

A billion choirs all sang at once,
A million Suns rose high,
Shining forth from countless worlds
In what had been the sky.

I looked again, now listening,
Within, without, I could not say
And in their midst a golden flute
Shone brighter than the day.

The songs it played came twirling out,
Sailing in the sky like ships,
A stream of nectar lifted them
Out from the Player's lips.

The flute piped out again once more,
Then the music danced away
But I can see it with my eyes
And hear it now, every day.

SHYAMASUNDAR

His eyes are like a lotus flower,
Poised above a crystal pool,
His arms are long and filled with power,
Like the Moon His hands are cool.

Soft radiance surrounds His face,
With forest flowers in His hair,
His body strong and filled with grace,
Imparts a fragrance to the air.

With secret lips of coral red
And eyebrows arched like Cupid's bow,
A peacock feather on His head
Above His garment's golden glow.

Surrounded by the forest creatures,
Beside a gently flowing stream,
The moonlight playing on His features,
Like a sweet enchanting dream.

He's standing there within our soul,
The Lord we left so long ago.
To please and serve Him is our goal,
His love is all we need to know.

O GOVINDA

O Lord the Sun's effulgence hides Your face,
The darkness of the night conceals Your eyes,
Your hands and legs reach all through outer space
And dawn displays Your beauty in the skies.

The rainbow shows the colors of Your dress,
The movements of the Moon reflect Your mind,
Your smiling is the cause of happiness
And love exists because You are so kind.

The rolling rivers flow forth from Your veins,
The clouds that fill the sky come from Your hair,
The seeds of life are watered by Your rains
And from Your breathing blows the mighty air.

My Lord You are the source of all I see,
Your movements are the passing days of time,
You are the resting place of all that be
And loving You has made my life sublime.

O Govinda within my heart,
Celestial herdsman, lotus-eyed One,
Your precious gift of love impart,
O You who stand behind the Sun.

Lyrics for *O Govinda* on the
Change of Heart CD produced by Michael Cassidy

SPEAK TO ME A DOCTRINE OF JOY

Speak to me a doctrine of joy,
Say that it includes a certain Girl and Boy

Immersed in thoughts of intimacy,
Upon the path of final ecstasy,

Where nearness leads to separation,
Intimate orgasmic meditation,

In which entwined intelligences,
Enwrap the silken bed, on which our senses

Wait for union, long for grace,
Worshipping the bliss of Their embrace.

Each perfumed breath and longing sigh,
Involves us in a love that will not die,

Their thoughts become our heartbeat drum
And thump the naked rhythm of things to come,

While flutes and pipes melodic trance,
Transport our souls, which then begin a dance,

In spinning circles, arcing up,
Her chalice filled with heady wine, Her cup

And He Her puppet tugs His strings,
A lute She plays, in the moon-lit night and sings

Songs of joy that live eternally,
A Boy and Girl bound in love but free.

JAYA RADHE

O golden Radharani fairest maid,
Wandering in a silent bamboo glade,
Like the pale and waning crescent Moon
Reflected on a shimmering lagoon.

Black, and moist with tears, Her restless eyes,
Search everywhere, while night conceals Her sighs
And gently floats the sound of Her lament,
Eternal song of love's embodiment.

Trembling shoulders graced with forest flowers,
Move in separation through the bowers,
Her shining garment's highest artistry,
Bedecked with glowing jewels of ecstasy,

An evolution of transcendent treasure,
Covered by the blouse of angry pleasure,
Searching in the woodland and the heather
For a glimpse of Krishna's peacock feather.

O lovely Radharani, golden ocean,
Dear most Gopi, Queen of lotus land,
Eternal Mother, emblem of devotion,
Please bless us with Your gentle loving hand.

CUPID'S SECRET

Vrindavan, the source
Of all beauty and radiance,
With bowers of lotus,
The seat of a jewel rare,
Secret garden enchanting
Where wanders in delicate dance,
Divine Loving Pair.

Soft moonbeams of silver
With nectar perfume the night air,
While peacocks like rainbows
And cuckoos sweet sing to enhance.
With garlands of ecstasy,
Circling the bamboo lair
And a distant flute song
Evergreen hearts does entrance.

His crown at Her feet,
Forest flowers in Her hair,
Attracting the heart of Cupid
Their secret glance,
Divine Loving Pair.

RASA DANCE

Soft silver moonbeams fill the autumn night
And twinkling stars bedeck the firmament,
With amethyst and pearls of cool delight,
While glowing dancers in rare ornament,

Draw graceful circles amidst the fragrant flowers,
Sweet zephyrs bear the song of frenzied bees
And black deer watch wide-eyed from sheltered bowers,
Within the hollows of the whispering trees.

With peacock feather rainbow on His head,
The gopis' hands upon His shoulders rest,
An enchanting flute-song through the night is spread
And on His feet the kunkum from their breasts.

Govinda dances with the milkmaids fair
And gently places flowers in their hair.

IMAGINE THE FLUTE

Imagine the flute,
So close to the lips that play it,
Caressing each note,
Breathing softly,
Empty to be filled,
An instrument,
Some bamboo
From the bank of a river,
Flowing endlessly,
Carefully prepared
To kiss those lips.

O what melodies, dance unending
Into the night,
What inspiration.
Imagine the flute,
Upon that mouth,
Singing songs
From the heart that holds it,
Full to overflowing.

Imagine the flute
At sunset in a forest,
Nimble fingers
Playing upon her,
While the honey Moon
Rains nectar from the sky.

JAMUNA

Listen, if you want to enjoy,
With society, family and friends,
Don't go near the Jamuna river,
Stay away from those lovely bends.

Where the moonlight shines upon
Sweet smiling, reddish, cunning lips,
No don't go there or you may be caught,
By those delicate fingertips.

If you're hoping to pass the time,
At home with children and mate,
Then beware of Vrindavan forest,
When the peacocks call and it's late.

But if you don't mind crying
And you aren't afraid of the truth,
You might consider meeting
At night, with a lotus-eyed youth.

If you're willing to travel blindly,
To give up the fight and surrender
Or live in a world that is hard,
With a heart that is open and tender,

Then don't say I didn't warn you,
If you end up a prisoner like me,
Wandering sadly, hopeless and lost,
A slave to the love of Hari.

81

I REMEMBER THE NIGHT WE FIRST MET

I remember the night we first met,
You were a mighty Lord beyond my knowing,
For I was a common person with no understanding yet,
Seeing You from a distance, something in me started growing.

You had a supreme power over our lives,
So I sought to serve You in some way.
I was taken into the kitchen of Your wives,
Cooking sweet dishes for You every day.

Sometimes I even imagined You were a child
And I nourished You from my heart,
Other times I dreamed fantasies so wild,
My strong emotions began to tear me apart.

Those around me saw my condition and knew
And so in Your garden on a summer night,
Arranged for me to meet alone with You,
I remember Your eyes in the silver starlight.

You instructed me in the confidence of love
And asked me to serve in Your private palace,
From my humble quarters I was taken above,
From a no one I was lifted up by Your grace.

In this way, You and I became friends,
Impossible but true, we sat for hours,
Discussing all manner of things, holding hands,
I forgot Your opulence, greatness and powers.

I REMEMBER THE NIGHT WE FIRST MET CONT'D

You became the companion of my soul,
The person with whom I shared every breath,
You gave me the vision to see things whole
And taught me that love does not fear death.

Then came the time You traveled far away,
On a mission of state, on some great journey,
For me each moment seemed a day,
Each night an endless void filled with yearning.

At last I was taken by Your smiling maids,
Who placed me in a blooming garden bower,
Adorned me with jeweled silks and gold brocades
And wove into my hair each fragrant flower.

A full Moon rose the hour we were wed,
With tears of joy my wondering eyes were wet
And as You led me to our wedding bed,
I again remembered the night we first met.

SWAN OF ENDLESS LOVE

I have swallowed Your universe,
Turning me upside down,
Orbits spinning in reverse.
A kaleidoscope of sound

Fills my head,
My ears are blind
And hear like eyes instead
Of groping in the mind.

Your visions have encompassed me,
Enwrapped and covered I,
A chrysalis of ecstasy,
On wings of grace I fly

Into Your realm of purest light,
Bright heart within the flame,
An ocean of divine delight
Within Your Holy Name.

O refuge of my pilgrim soul,
Immortal realm of grace,
I die a sleep so wonderful
And awake to see Your face.

A million tongues in unison
Lick nectar from Your lips,
The rays of an immortal Sun
Drink dew in tiny sips

From lotus flowers bright in hue,
Upon each golden stream,
The swan of endless love for You,
Is swimming in my dream.

A REFUGEE

The forest echoes with a melody,
An early morning sylvan rhapsody,

A flute and lute in perfect harmony,
Like words combined in rhyming prosody.

The drifting clouds like waves of ebony,
Rejoice their thunder's rolling euphony,

Outpouring notes like teardrops watery
And treetops rustle with the symphony.

The peacocks fly with all their finery
Around the sheltered bower's reverie.

There twirling round and round in ecstasy,
As if, in some enchanting fantasy,

The Pair entwined in dancing unity,
Like some great spinning spiral galaxy,

A loving dance of perfect purity,
The two in one Eternal Deity,

Unfolding as an endless trilogy,
Embracing all in Their festivity.

Now having seen this Gorgeous Effigy
And hearing this delightful eulogy,

You'll understand my painful malady
And why I live my life a refugee.

SURRENDERED TO YOUR BLUE

Pierced by the darts of Kama it is no wonder
That my gentle heart has been torn asunder
Over time, losing its natural hue
Shaken again and again by bolts and thunder,
Its crimson pride has surrendered to Your blue.

Through Your garden I ran, with wonder filled
And drunken on love, the perfume Your flowers spilled
Swept me beyond the clutter at my feet,
Instructing me in Your ways with its sweet
Fragrance, a drug to which I ever thrilled.

Your teasing eyes watching from beyond,
Starlight reflected upon my thoughtful pond,
Swam upon its waters, a graceful swan,
Wisdom rose within me, a golden dawn,
Turning our passion into a deeper bond.

The Moon of Your face bathed me in its glance,
The sound of Your flute taught me how to dance,
Our longing looks educated my soul,
Waiting for You somehow made me whole
And I began to glow with Your radiance.

SURRENDERED TO YOUR BLUE CONT'D

You removed the arrows one by one.
I became Your Moon and You my Sun,
Kissing in the shadows of our eclipse,
I bear the marks upon me from Your lips,
Preparing to consummate what love begun.

I am almost ready for Your embrace,
See You only, intent upon Your face,
Feel Your touch awake and in my dreams,
Know You love me no matter how life seems,
Every moment has always been Your grace.

LISTEN, THE NIGHT WEEPS

I am waiting patiently
In the shadows of Your heart,
Breathless at the grove
Where our love was planted.
My tears are so cold,
Like precious stones
They cover the naked ground.
Calling Your name again
And again, and once more,
Pride flees from desperation.
Touch my body! It quivers,
Broken beneath Your hand.
Our promises have cut
The threads of my mind.
Willing victim, I always wait,
Watching for a sign.
Listen! The night weeps!
Does the Moon see this
Sad scene of fading dreams,
Growing thin in sympathy?
Hush that choking melody,
Fitful bird, heart pounding
At the empty perfumed air,
Beating captive wings about.
Laugh morning, again, and mock
My sorrow with your glare.
Blind the eyes that cannot see
Burn hot until ashen night
Descends again to bring me hope,
A hope that will never die.

LAMP IN A WINDLESS PLACE

These words are smoke
Rising from the fire
Blazing in my heart
Lamp-black from the Truth,
An oblation for the gods,
The flesh of my being
On the altar of life.

This sacrifice rises skyward,
Raining tears upon a garden
Within my heart, a creeper grows:
Delicate plant of love,
A vine reaching for the Divine
Grows slowly outside my hut.

In a sacred grove of trees,
On the banks of a holy river,
I sit before the fire
Pouring butter upon the coals,
Fasting, waiting in silence,
A lamp in a windless place,
Burns to see the Truth
Speak with a tongue of flame.

ASCENDING LIKE A FLAME

Ascending like a flame at night,
My soul in robes of dazzling light,

Licks the sparkling stars in space,
Shooting beams of joy and grace.

A cosmic Aurora Borealis,
Lamp within a crystal chalice,

Incandescent incarnation,
Burns the oil of transformation.

Like a lotus upon a pond,
Rooted here but bloomed beyond,

My spirit climbs in curling arcs,
A blazing torch emitting sparks,

Which crack the blue and strike the peak.
The lightning bolts of truth I speak

Split the clouds again and again,
Until they cry their seedling rain.

Then as the Sun breaks into view,
I form a rainbow, born anew.

Bursting into flames of love,
My soul ascends to Your realms above.

A LOTUS I BLOSSOM

O my Beloved I long for Your touch,
The wind blows Your name across the sea
Everyone says that I love You too much
But too much is never enough for me.

My Darling I see You in every face,
Their eyes, twin gates to Your mystery,
Shine like stars in the vastness of space,
Sparks from the endless Sun of Your beauty.

My Dearest I hear Your voice in my ear,
When they tell me our love can never be,
Whispering messages, calming my fear
Filling my heart with Your ecstasy.

Sweet Lover I dream of a kiss from Your lips
My dream is an endless fantasy,
From the well of Your mouth I am drinking deep sips,
Like a lotus I blossom infinitely.

O my Beloved, I live in the light
And wait for the day when again I see
Your body with mine in the endless night,
Loving You into eternity.

THIS IS MY YOGA

I have done the Yoga of sitting still,
Holding the empty begging bowl of space,
Stopping the river of thought with the dam of will,
Standing on one foot in a holy place.

I have become the effulgence of limitless light,
A drop merging in the ocean of endless bliss,
Beyond the pull of gravity or night,
That which is eternal, thou art this.

I have become the cosmos turning around,
The hub of a wheel, revolving everything,
Point in the womb of space, primeval sound.
I have met the Angels and learned to sing.

I have been born in every form of life,
Ascending from slime to the golden mountain peak,
Peaceful one moment, then torn by hatred and strife.
All this, yet there is something I still seek:

O love of my soul, I would trade it all,
For a moment gazing into Your lotus eyes.
There is no other god, no big or small,
Only fervent love under moon-lit skies.

Illusion winks but beauty has made me blind.
This true love is the yoga of my heart
Near or far it grows within my mind.
I am Your self; You are my missing part.

Blindly, I run searching for Your feet,
Crazy, O yes, a madness so divine,
That bees have never tasted such a sweet
Or drunkards such intoxicating wine.

This is my yoga, a hunger for Your kiss
And if they ask me when we will be one,
I cry and answer: "What and such love miss?"

I am a spark from Your eternal Sun.
I am a song and You the meadowlark.
I am the rosy hue upon Your dawn.
I am Your lover, waiting in the dark.

WAITING WITH ALL MY MIGHT

I have been waiting so long,
My love has grown quiet.
Like night with no stars,
I am expectation
Turned in upon itself.
No longer looking,
Silence tells me secrets
I cannot share.
The endless distance
Of my heart,
Opens dreaming seconds,
Bright flashes of light
Thunder my longing.
I am not a mountain
Waiting silently alone
Watching silly flowers
Nod as if they know.
I am love incarnate,
Waiting to be loved,
Longing for the touch,
Infinite consummation,
Waiting with all my might.

LOVING STONE

My Beloved, I think of You throughout the day,
Busy with a million things that must be done.
They flow over me like a flooding river,
A turbulent stream of endless change,
Where I am a rock at the bottom.
I am a stone that cannot be moved.
I am a patient boulder submerged
But inside I have a secret life.
Like a geode I am filled with jewels,
Crystal seeds You planted in my center,
Purple reminders of the way we kissed.
Glowing in the dark of my silent heart,
A mystic fire transforms my clay
Something burns my rock to gems.
Some pressure recreates my being,
Until I reflect each facet of You.
And when I am perfectly bright,
You will reach down into the current
And find me waiting alone.
You will break me open darling
And see the heart of a loving stone.

FADED FLOWERS

Oh hear my Beloved I am waiting,
Where the moonbeams are kissing the dew,
In the darkness but anticipating
The time when Your promise comes true.

I searched near and far in the forest,
A place You'd be happy to lie,
Now I wait for Your footsteps my dearest
But from crying my eyes have gone dry.

The flowers I picked have all faded,
Sweet lotus and jasmine so fine,
In the strands of my hair I had braided,
While thinking of making You mine.

Where the curtains of creepers are waving,
There a waterfall flows down the hill,
Summer breezes increasing my craving
And the black deer stand perfectly still.

The swans all were sure You were coming,
The peacocks pretended to hear,
What the bumblebees sang in their humming,
They all said You'd surely appear.

Still I sit in the night broken-hearted,
You may come if you ever get bored,
Here I sit where I was when we parted,
In the night, in a forest, O Lord.

TWIRLING LOVERS

Rumor has it that Bhaktis are not so bright,
Sentimentalists, lost in human emotion,
Crying with dancing peacocks late at night,
Swelling with tears like the tides of Varuna's ocean.

Seeing the thunderclouds pour, they cry again,
Hearing a flute in the call of a whippoorwill,
Their sobs could be joy or a jilted lover's pain,
Drunken, they drink but cannot get their fill.

While frowning scholars correct their grammar and style,
Linguistic vultures, picking the carrion's bones.
The blessed ignore the barbs with a blissful smile,
Unable to hear above their joyful groans.

From the desert of speculation where they were bred,
Dry philosophers count the grains of sand
And argue on water with rocks in the riverbed,
Concluding that birds cannot fly because they land.

They lick the jar to taste the honey within,
Define the journey from where they have begun,
Doubt the soul, writing libraries on the skin,
And state their personal view that all are one

But meanwhile, twirling lovers charm the stars,
To the beat of an unseen drum, they start the dance,
While Devas throw flowers from their celestial cars
And the rising Moon becomes Govinda's glance.

GAUR HARI

O Lord your name a song so sweet
Is a whisper soft to eager ears,
Who crying seek Your soothing feet
And wash Your temple with their tears.

Your blackish eyes, a lotus whorl,
Attract the heart of a swan-like mind,
Who searching for a single pearl
A priceless treasure is blest to find.

Drink deep, O men of piety,
The nectar of the Holy Name,
Dive into the sea of ecstasy
Bow down before the cleansing flame.

Surrender all you falsely hold
And raise your arms in joyful dance,
With He who shines like molten gold
Rise up and feel His loving glance.

O Lord Chaitanya, fairest One,
Your full Moon rising in the skies,
Outshines the beauty of the Sun
And fills with love our searching eyes.

THE IMAGE OF DESCENDING GRACE

The simple-minded miss the point,
The symbol-minded are saying,
Letters themselves cannot anoint,
The form on which they are essaying.

They are, in fact, reflected glory,
Shining from a distant realm,
Hints that tell a cryptic story,
A ship with mystery at the helm.

Images playing on the wall,
A cinema projected from afar,
Reflect the Source, including all,
With fragments gleaming from each star.

The layers of coded meaning shine,
Concentric rings, the octaves sing,
Threads of a warp and woof Divine,
The sacred meaning of everything,

Is woven into a tapestry,
A silken fabric draped on space,
A rainbow robe of He and She,
Made in the image of descending grace.

The mandala within our eyes,
Reveals the planets' slow ellipse,
Eternal life that never dies,
Is visible and then eclipsed.

And in the yantra of our shape,
Dynamic and static articulate,
Forms transcendent that we ape,
Unconscious, we transubstantiate.

A floating bridge between two worlds,
Metaphors in a foreign land,
A banner whose meaning is unfurled,
Upon our forehead and our hands.

We wear our history on our face,
With petals wrapped, our lotus heart,
Exudes perfume, our hidden grace,
Wants to bloom, our eternal part.

Lies within, yet tells the truth,
Is hidden there in all we see,
Our true self, an eternal youth,
Revealed at last in ecstasy.

I UNDERSTAND YOUR GREATNESS

I understand that Your greatness
Is a defense against our freedom,
A fortress of illusory boundaries
Which the loving eye sees not,
Built on the foundation of our ignorance.
I want to become like You.
Like You, I want to love too much,
Until thoughts are a spider's web
I brush from my face
And tears are a river in spate,
Cutting canyons in my granite heart.
I want to not want to want
But to want to give and give,
To expand Your love by accepting
Expecting nothing in return.
I want to return to Your embrace
And shine that grace moon-like,
Rising quite drunk on Your sweetness,
To pour forth Your succor
And suckle at the Holy Breast,
That every starving soul be fed.
I know Your greatness is a veil
For those who will not love
But to me it is a silver sail
On a ship that drifts into Your cove,
An island where You wait for me,
To hold me in Your ecstasy.

HEAD FIRST

I know there is pure water in the well
But my pail is too small
To raise it to the surface.
The rope is too short, I can tell
It would be easy to fall
Into that dark and unknown place.

I can hear the echo of my voice
And smell the freshness of the spring,
The musty scent of Earth,
Around me a chorus as songbirds rejoice,
Flitting messages on the wing,
The spring bubbles at me with mirth.

Teasing me, the waters call my name,
They know all my secret places,
Giggling droplets that once were rain,
They murmur of a loving game,
Lotus lips on smiling faces
Wearing away at my earthly pain.

I know there is only one way,
Only one path to taste this bliss,
Headfirst I leap without a sound,
A teardrop learning how to play,
I feel the wetness of their kiss,
Love is the only way to drown.

SECRET MESSAGES

Flirting with us through a billion eyes,
Teasing us in each disguise,
Full Moon of love You rise
And hypnotize
The wise.
The trees
Bend their knees,
To smell Your fragrant breeze,
Blooming with Your ecstasies,
Mindless rivers rush to meet the seas.
Flocks of birds cavorting through the air,
Write letters hinting You are there
And decorate Your hair,
A loving pair,
They share.
Your kiss,
The endless sweetness,
Encrypted in all that is,
Containing the secret messages,
A note of passion written by Your bliss.
Beloved You pretend to be away,
To hear us whisper every day,
To listen as we pray,
Love is, we say,
The only way.
Delight,
Black and white,
Images crossing night,
Shining from beyond our sight,
Embrace conducted at the speed of light.

YOUR SWEETNESS

Reaching out with fingers of delight,
I grasp You with tendrils of light,

Wrapping my soft leaves around Your bud,
Pulsing with the flow of Your green blood

I am Your friend in a fragrant bed,
Intertwined, my roots within Your head

And Your branches clinging to my own,
This fragrance is the flower we have grown.

We feel the footsteps of the bee,
Touching us in the midst of ecstasy,

With the pollen of our flowers on his face,
This divine drinks the honey of our embrace.

We are roses growing in the wild,
Enmeshed with Your petals I am beguiled,

By the colors shining on Your cheek,
Your sweetness is the treasure that I seek.

WITHOUT AND WITHIN

When my senses are turned without,
I am a swaggering man,
Poking and prodding, in and out,
Taking pleasure where I can.

With my tongue I penetrate
Each succulent orifice,
With every flavor I am intimate,
Each sensation gives me bliss.

My fingers fondle every surface,
My eyes caress each shape,
My ears reach out to every place,
My senses live to rape.

Each passing thought, a new delight,
I am never satisfied,
Searching for pleasures day and night,
Until I look inside.

Within I find myself a girl,
In silk and satin clad,
With pouting lips and hair in curls,
Dreaming of a handsome Lad.

A Prince who lives in a magic land,
A Hero who loves only me,
Deep of voice and soft of hand,
He wants to set me free.

A slayer of wicked beasts,
He searches for my jail,
He rises glorious in the east,
His ship sails with a billowing sail.

I know He's coming and so I wait,
A prisoner in my cell,
When the Moon is full and night is late,
I wait for Him to break the spell.

Beast and maiden, girl and man,
Without, within, like night and day,
One lives to take all that he can,
One waits to be taken far away.

FLOATING ON A SEA OF BLISS

Each day I feed the gaping hole
But still it does not make me whole.
No matter how much more I give it,
It always remains an empty pit.

Every flavor taste or spice,
Fuels my need for another slice,
As every breath of air I take,
Cannot, my need for breathing slake.

And try as I will to stay awake,
Every night sleep overtakes.
My senses pull like restless steeds,
Pressing me to fulfill their needs,

While the maniac mind demands to know,
Where we have been, where we will go,
A crazy monkey in a tree,
Wherever I go he follows me

And intellect, my so-called friend,
Defers to logic in the end,
Restating the problem as the conclusion,
That know-it-all promotes delusion.

So if you wonder where I've gone
Or what I rest my self upon,
In a world of danger, based on flux,
My consciousness has found the crux.

Near an island outside space,
Upon a life-raft labeled "grace,"
I'm floating on a sea of bliss,
Beyond the asylum where randomness

Has driven the inmates all insane,
Where they take birth again and again.
I'm drifting upon the loving ocean,
Where the rescue ship S.S. Devotion

Plies the waters and endless shoals,
Looking for matter-weary souls
And when they throw that rope to me,
This time I'll hold it eternally.

TURNING TOWARD PERFECTION

Fluorescent forms glow in the lap of night,
In the nether regions between dawn and twilight,

Lines blur between one form and another,
As each thing seeks to find its missing lover.

The hard lines of day fade to extinction,
The eagle eye fails to find distinctions,

As ears echo with pulsing reverberations,
Bodies seek release in wild gyrations.

The mad Moon with cyclic fingertips,
Pours her honey into waiting lips.

Sweet libations served in crystal spheres,
Stored in curving bottles many years,

The spirits take birth again to dance once more,
Another twirling walk across the floor.

The notes, a path, lead to a sacred grotto,
A spell forgotten, unwinds from the vibrato.

This ritual is older than the Earth,
The universe sang these songs before its birth.

TURNING TOWARD PERFECTION CONT'D

The flaming need that sparks this shadow play,
Burned before its sparks fell into clay,

Rode across infinitude and space,
Cascaded over mountains' stony face.

This need smolders deeper than any sea,
This dance began in ancient eternity.

It is our deeper self in search of joy,
A blossoming Girl dreaming of the Perfect Boy,

A man ready to die for his lover's glance,
Our souls spinning in the cosmic disco dance.

Perfect spirals turning toward perfection,
Eternal spirits tasting resurrection,

Drinking in the tavern with no shame,
Drunken on the Beloved's Holy Name.

Fluorescent forms dance in their delight,
Between illusion and reflected light.

DANCING FOOTSTEPS ARE ALL I HEAR

Our dancing drives me crazy,
The rest of the time I am lazy

But spinning in circles of bliss
Is the purpose of consciousness?

In the musical orbits of night,
Spins the secret of our delight

And twirling at last in the sky,
Is where we go when we die.

In Your perfumed hair, my dear,
The gardens of heaven are near

And Your orbiting form is on fire,
With tongues of celestial desire.

Like a comet with love in Your tail,
I follow your orbit, a trail,

With the wind of Your breath in my ear,
Your dancing footsteps are all I hear.

EVER SINCE WE MET

Ever since we met I have been restless,
Unable to focus on any goal
And all my knowing now is useless,
My life is spinning out of control.

Ever since we kissed my lips are moving,
Speaking words I cannot understand,
Crying in my dream about our loving,
Reaching out all night to touch Your hand.

Everything appears to have a meaning,
Pretends to have a simple plan
But those illusions are simply screening
Messages written for me by Your hand.

Silence on my lips a red pretending,
Teardrops on my cheek a would-be rain,
The clouds a love that crushes never ending,
My heartbeat the prayer to see You once again.

THE MIGHTY WIND IS BUT A BREATH

The spinning Earth, a turquoise liquid drop,
Stays in orbit with no hook or prop,
A circle in a cycle that won't stop.

The Sun, ignited by some ancient flame,
Burns itself but always shines the same,
It is a tiger darkness cannot tame.

The honeyed Moon with crescent nails and lips,
Embraces Sun and Earth with her ellipse,
Sky-pump in the well of her eclipse.

Divine islands, whose distance is the most,
The sentry stars stand twinkling at their post,
Supporting life with light this Heavenly Host.

Time is awake while all others sleep,
From the mountain peaks, to the ocean deep,
Into every corner of life it will creep.

The mighty wind, held by greater space,
And held again by even greater grace,
Is but a breath from Vishnu's endless face.

THE MEANING OF DOUBT

I am surrounded by their doubts,
They are sneering with undisguised contempt,
And each is the servant of a piece of ignorance.

They stare at me with cold reptilian eyes,
Observing my every move like birds of prey,
They know this game and taunt me,
Hoping to be the one to find my weakness.

And night is the place where they congregate,
Not the turquoise night with stars and Moon,
Not the vast unlimited night with constellations,
Not the purple night with a flute in the distance,
Their night is a dead and empty void,
With no sounds, no hope, no love and no escape.

In that night, even day is black with smog and smoke
And so I sit in their midst with one-pointed concentration,
Remembering the Sun who gave me life and is my Lord.

Crying tears that would burn their skin like poison,
Remembering, remembering, remembering our love,
Waiting endlessly for the day You will return,
Sita says: "Now I know the meaning of doubt."

YOU LIT THE FIRE WITH MY TEARS

When the flame of Your love burns low,
Alone in the third watch of the night
And the impending gloom is all I know,
My wick flickers in the dying light.

I begin to whisper Your name,
As tears drop like a sudden rain
But that water ignites the flame,
Water becoming fire seems insane.

Yet somehow it is so and You
Are suddenly there embracing me,
The night has passed and morning's blue
Eyes, flecked with silver filigree,

Open in a sudden burst of light,
Peaking up in the east, Your orb,
Shatters the fetters that bound me to night,
Pouring more love than I can absorb.

O how petty and small my fears,
How quickly I forget Your face,
So You lit the fire with my tears
And now I'll never forget Your grace.

KISSED BY KRISHNA

Like flickering green lights, the waving leaves
Flash hidden messages across the trees,

Direct transmissions of code to our cells,
A branched semaphore from the Sun, that tells

Each carbon chain the proper sequence,
Photons sparkle, a chain of sequins

Programming darkness to become what is,
Master program, run by photosynthesis.

The stuff of life arranged by luminous will,
Leaps from light to life through chlorophyll,

Then sends the binary message to our eyes,
Projecting visions of distant paradise.

Racing across the emptiness of space,
Flashes of light reflect upon our face

And lucent waves of love rise in our heart,
Kissed by Krishna, though we are far apart.

BLUE THUNDER BLIND

You came to me in the night
When I could not refuse,
In the fickle candlelight,
With Your dark enchanting hues.

What poor girl could see You
Without giving up her pride?
So my white has turned to blue,
When I think of how You lied.

Sometimes I even wonder
If You're just within my mind
But my heart still pounds like thunder
And Your love has made me blind.

The day has started sleeping
While the Moon is losing weight.
There's a secret You've been keeping
But I only cry of late.

So excuse me if I'm rambling
Like a madman in a wood.
After all, love's just like gambling
And You always knew I would.

A FOREST I CALL HOME

I can hear the distant laughter,
Within a forest I have known,
Calling me to follow after,
Standing on this cliff alone,

Sylvan music steals my ear,
Pipes in concert from within,
Waves across a rolling pasture,
A chorus of painted birds begin

Flying in patterns through my sky,
Secret letters form and fade,
Turning within, the light, my eye,
Shadows moving across my shade,

Dance me sunrise, sing me night,
Rise within my moonbeam ship,
Sail on seas of my delight,
Drown on the shore of my Love's lip.

Their whispers trail into my hollow
And deep within my forest roam,
They beckon me and I will follow,
To a forest I call home.

BREAKING MY MIND

There You go again, breaking my mind,
I know it was just a cane for the blind

But You are a rude and unfriendly guest,
Smashing the bed wherever You rest.

Like a giant that nothing fits,
You break our tiny lives to bits,

Spoiling our wives with love unending,
Because You are all, You're always pretending.

Lying again, with no explanation,
You tease us within our imagination

But since I am blind You can't fool me,
I smell you in every mystery,

I hear Your footsteps without fail
And read Your sub-atomic Braille,

With fingertips that do not touch,
You try too hard and do too much,

An over-achieving Deity,
How dare You try to run from me,

You broke my life but fixed my heart,
So now we'll never be apart.

KRISH NA

You are the greatest negation,
The oldest star,
Collapsed in upon Yourself,
Endless contradiction,
Sucking us relentlessly into Your core,
Into the heart of Your Being.

Your gravity has become attraction,
Pulling us to play
Hide and seek in the Heavens.
Flautist, You flaunt Your power,
Sucking Your big toe,
Cosmic baby, floating
Upon the waters You cried.

Blinking another universe,
Who can believe Your lies,
When all of them are true.

And in our real-time dreams,
Waking to see Your face
Is the final fantasy
Reality has to offer,
Before everything is again reduced
To galactic wet-dreams.

No big-bang here,
Just a whisper in the night,
I love You,
The greatest negation.

YOU ARE SMILING FROM THE MOON

I have a question to ask, my love, but first,
How may I serve You, do You have a desire?
Is there anything for which You hunger or thirst?
Make me Your consultant and we will conspire

To serve each others' joy in subtle ways,
I will feed You sweetmeats from my hand,
I will script the scenes of loving plays,
Then turn the ending different than we planned.

I see my lips reflected in Your eyes,
Where You are swimming naked in the night,
In midnight pools but then to my surprise,
We're walking beneath a sky of scattered starlight.

When that becomes a beach at moonrise tide,
With lapping waves splashing at our toes,
Then suddenly I blink and look inside,
Where You are smiling from the Moon that rose.

THIS GREAT LOVE

This great love must be You again,
Overflowing from my tiny heart.
These words are an eternal refrain,
That have no end and never start.

There is plenty here for all to drink,
The world could swim in a drop of You.
My eyes cannot close or blink,
From moment to moment all is new.

Evergreen in a forest growing,
The plant of my devotion blooms
And seeks the lamp where You are glowing,
In sheltered bowers, fragrant rooms.

Where maidens decorate Your seat,
Hoping You will join them soon.
With fragrant incense and perfume sweet,
They await You like the rising Moon.

BLACK DELIGHT

Near sunset, in a forest, I ventured out alone.
On an unknown trail, dense and overgrown.

Across a clearing, I heard the Moon arise,
Not quite silent, she blinked before my eyes.

Half dressed, in a robe of ochre cloud,
She bent before me, surrounded by a crowd

Of sycophantic stars, that serve her feet
And bent before her, just to taste the sweet

Nectar flowing slowly from her laugh,
For she was naked from her evening bath.

Then slowly I sensed a presence on the trail
And saw the flicking motion of a tail.

An ebony serpent shining in the light,
Curved toward me like a wave of black delight.

Then suddenly, the serpent rose and stood,
Drawing a bamboo flute up to His hood,

The snake blew melodies into the dusk,
Which mingled with the jasmine and the musk

And like a puppet, my feet began to move,
As that serpent jazz man found His groove.

The swaying trees stepped beyond their roots,
Like rows of frenzied dancers in silver boots,

We leapt into a syncopated line,
Turning madly in a delirium divine,

While overhead angelic beings flew,
Showering flowers and intoxicating dew.

In widening circles, filling the endless space,
An orchestra appeared, the serpent's face

Was visible now and all who saw it cried:
"This is no snake!" Their eyes opened wide,

As Shyamasundar danced into their midst,
Rushing from one to another, He kissed

Their lips and spun each one just so,
While I, among them turning, began to glow

And this is the tale of how I came to be,
How one dark night I became a galaxy.

I SAW YOU AGAIN TODAY

I saw you again today from a distance
But You could not see me
And I could have used Your assistance,
Could have tasted Your ecstasy.

But You had another agenda,
Some distraction had caught Your eye,
So I looked away, a pretender,
While You looked at me asking: Why?

The moment slowed down like it does
When the details are going to be dreamed,
Clear at the center, the edges go fuzz,
Forever went by, so it seemed.

Hide and go seek is Your favorite game,
Tag you're it, I can see in Your eyes,
Pretending that You and I are the same,
While hinting at paradise.

Hiding in sunset, You wink in the night,
Kissing my cheek before dawn,
Just when I think my timing is right,
You laugh one more time and are gone.

EVEN IF

Even if I never see You again,
Never feel Your eyelashes upon my cheek,
Even if all I ever know is pain,
Day after day and week after lonely week.

Even if I never kiss Your lips,
While the cowardly Moon hides in a jasmine grove
And a madness from which I cannot recover grips,
My mind, my heart, pretending to speak on love.

Even if the dreams I stand upon,
The very foundation on which my life is made,
Falls to pieces and all I know is gone,
If the rest of life is a useless masquerade.

And even if light turns to dark and down is up,
If I wander alone in a desert never ending,
With no relief, not a drop of water in my cup,
In a world gone mad with violence and pretending.

Even if You decide to never return,
To leave me in the night unseen, unheard,
I promise You our love will always burn
And I will call Your name with my last word.

DARK LORD

O Dark Lord, You have hidden Your Self in the night
And though I have seen Your footprints upon the trail,
Your exact location remains a mystery
But no doubt involves some other sultry female,
In whose arms You are taking delight,
So that I wonder who my rival could be.

Of course it doesn't matter, You have so many,
More numerous than the stars that light the sky,
Yet fool that I am, I seek You anyway,
For no good reason, I cannot tell you why,
I run at a wealthy man waving my penny,
Dreaming that You may come to me some day.

For I have made a feast of sweets my love
And woven fragrant flowers in my hair,
Our bed perfumed with sandal, jasmine and musk,
Was made by me, for passion, with great care.
The night is still and Venus stands above,
Moist and shining from her bath at dusk.

Yes, I am waiting now and always will,
I feel You near within this forest glade,
The lamps I lit will burn now for a while,
I strain my eyes to see You in the shade.
My heart is pounding with each ecstatic thrill,
As the crescent Moon arises like Your smile.

YOU ARE HIDING

I know You are hiding somewhere just out of sight,
Where Your dark beauty is obscured by night.

I hear Your flute in the songs of the nightingale,
Weaving Your love notes into her haunting scale.

I see Your footprints on the trail ahead of me,
Your fingerprints upon apparent serendipity.

My heart calls Your name, O Lover mine,
I see Your mind in a spider web's design,

I hear Your music when the sleeping world is dark,
I feel Your passion in the trilling of the lark.

I cannot desert You, cannot stay, cannot flee,
I cannot live in bondage or bear to set You free.

I cannot always have You nor stand to let You go,
I know You but don't know how much I know.

You are smiling somewhere just beyond my reach,
Waves whisper Your names to the empty beach.

I see Your smile upon the faces of the blind,
You are waiting somewhere in the shadows of my mind.

YOU ARE HIDING CONT'D

You are on the mountain peak I somehow cannot climb,
You are in a forest, on a planet out of time.

You are in my heart, sitting closer than I know,
You are the ocean into which my rivers flow.

You are my Beloved in a passionate embrace,
You are the tear rolling slowly down my face.

I know You have never left me, yet I cry,
To hold You closer than the eyelid to my eye.

I want You nearer than the thoughts within my brain,
Nearer than the blood in my pulsing jugular vein.

I know You are waiting to remove Your disguise,
Until the look of love is just perfect in my eyes

And though I feel Your lashes brush my cheek,
You are still out of sight when I peek.

THE GLANCE OF SHYAMASUNDAR

From the bushes, eyes are watching me,
Hiding there to veil their ecstasy.

Restless feet, twinkling ankle bells,
Reddish footprints lead to hidden dells.

This forest is a secret place,
One can only enter it by grace

And once within cannot ever leave,
Waiting is the method to receive,

Crying is the rain the flowers need,
Love is the blood that lovers bleed,

Fragrance from the rose is Her desire,
The Moon rises up a little higher.

Each moment is eternity,
Anything we want infinity

And here in this emerald sanctuary,
Nothing happens that is ordinary,

Nothing lasts, yet all is endless,
Each is alone but no one friendless.

Then music comes from a hidden player,
A lute begins to play like a whispered prayer,

THE GLANCE OF SHYAMASUNDAR CONT'D

Radha from Her chamber is lamenting,
Krishna hears Her notes somewhere repenting.

He pipes up, His bamboo flute is wailing,
Her staccato fingers are assailing.

He cannot resist and madly rushes,
She hears His footsteps, strumming, luscious

Symphonies resound throughout the forest,
Gopis giggle, glancing from their secret nest,

Peacocks scream and dance in syncopation,
The night explodes with joy and wild vibration.

From their hiding places, lovers madly rushing,
Crying, singing, moaning, just like fountains gushing.

In a clearing Madhusudana is standing,
While a million gopi girls rush demanding:

"Dance with us, O Lover never ending,
Convince us that Your love is real and not pretending."

Then millions of Gopalas fill the endless forest,
As every gopi leads Him to her love nest

And just as I am starting to feel lonely,
I feel the glance of Shyamasundar on me.

WHAT CAN I SAY?

What can I say about this longing?
It is a sky full of distant stars,
Twinkling or my eyes are blinking,
Flashing messages or I am dreaming.

Wanting You consumes my days,
Night tries to distract my attention
But I sweep it away each morning.
Webs spun in the dark are crooked.

This is not the life I had expected.
You stole the corners of my square room,
Spun my compass and made me wobble.
My orbit has become eccentric.

If I died for You, yet live,
Glued my broken heart into a cup
And drank my sorrow with cream and sugar,
Celebrating my opportunity to miss You,

If I dressed in a negligee of whispers
And danced in a frenzy with Your name,
Until the spinning galaxies got tired,
Would You who are never away come closer?

I am at a loss to describe,
The exponential effect of kisses,
Held as I am by Your loving embrace,
This longing for You constantly increases.

SPRING OF ETERNAL LOVE

Because my heart was broken open,
I cannot close my eyes
And seeing sorrow keep on hoping
To share a vision of paradise.

The secret, of course, is easy to know,
Love is the gentle power,
Which gives the soul strength to grow
And selfishness is the tower

In which the princess is locked away
Waiting for her Prince,
Hoping He will arrive some day
But still not quite convinced.

Another riddle is endless longing,
The fear of empty space,
Which love fills up with light belonging
To vision of the Beloved's face.

Because my rock was rent asunder,
Light shines through the crack,
Lightning hit and so did thunder,
There is no turning back

But when the stone is finally crushed,
The truth is a tender thing,
A stream of crystal feeling gushed,
The sound of a bubbling spring.

A tear on the blushing cheek of a maid,
A pool in a hidden grove,
That by a broken heart was made,
The spring of eternal love.

TIME TO GO HOME

I am surrounded by shining friends,
Just the other side of my mind,
They are laughing and playing,
Calling me to join them.
I hear whispers in the distance,
Inviting and cajoling.
Gentle fingers tug my heart
Lead me to secret gardens,
Bathe me in sparkling waters,
Dressing me in gold and jewels,
Feathers in my tangled hair.
My head is resting on the lap
Of loving friends, I almost hear
Feelings more real than thoughts.
There are more Moons than we see,
More Suns than you can count.
I am playing with the Devas,
Children on a cosmic playground,
Play hide and seek and I am it.
Ollie ollie all free,
Time to go home.

THE EPIC STRUGGLE

This struggle transcends the weathered pages
Of ancient tomes passed down by sages,

The epic stories that carried our past
Into the future of a present at last,

A battle waged over thousands of years,
A plot convoluted by tongues and ears,

Twisted by destiny's laws from the start,
Enmeshed in the passionate human heart.

Divine voices are trying to reach us,
Ancient sages would like to discuss

The subtle nuances of truth in action,
The ultimate sources of satisfaction

But we are distracted on pathways that wind,
Taught by the foolish and led by the blind,

Forgetful, bewildered, herded like sheep,
We bleat in anxiety, toss in our sleep,

Yet waking is facing the evil alone,
For our armies are scattered and we are but one.

A tree in a storm, on a hill, in a night,
A ranger on paths with no map and no light,

This is the truth of the stories of yore,
This is the fight we have taken birth for.

THE DREAM OF LOVE IS LIFE

I have been holding the dream of love in my heart,
Walking with water cupped in my hands,
Trying not to spill a precious drop,
Hoping the image will never fade.
Your lips whisper in my dreams,
Speaking the language of healing joy,
You live where music comes from.
Red silk stitched into my fabric,
We are sewn into a web of threads,
Golden strands of inner connection.
You have embroidered me with stars,
Spangled my mind with jasmine kisses,
Rained upon me hillside heaven,
Risen, the iris Moon of my eye,
Until I see every precious soul.
Dew drops on flower petals ripple,
Night vapor condensed as breath,
Holding this in a glass of silver light,
Trying to walk without falling,
I carry Your child within me,
I bear the dawning Sun inside.
Daughter of night's purple robe,
Lover with honey dripping down.
Everything is sacred with love,
Touching invisibly at the center,
The dream of love is life.

THE EARTH CAME TO ME

I had a dream and the Earth came to me,
With tear-filled eyes she gazed in sympathy,

At the plight of her children, quarreling in anger,
To see so many little ones in danger.

She showed me how each heart is a part of her,
She took me to a time when love was pure.

In that sweet vision, everyone was free
But all agreed to live in harmony.

Rulers fed their people before they ate,
No beggar was ever alone at the palace gate.

Men of power bowed with humility,
Praying to use their strength with sincerity.

Beautiful women inspired with their grace,
Teachers of love, with wisdom on their face

And everyone walked safely with no fear,
Music and laughter echoed in every ear.

Truth was law and promises were kept,
Nothing dangerous waited, lied or crept.

The elderly were honored, loved and safe,
No child was ever abandoned, alone, a waif.

The Earth asked me to share this vision of peace,
She cried and pleaded for the fighting to cease.

We wept together and prayed it will be so,
Now, share this dream with others so they will know.

THE HEROES OF EROS

Long before the waters froze,
In polar caps and glacial ice,
A group of celestial beings arose,
Sent here from some paradise.

Beyond all sorrow and all woes,
They grew on Earth in constant bliss,
Wisdom lived among them, those
Who knew them tasted happiness.

But gradually their sweet repose,
Was shattered by invading hordes,
With whom they were forced to come to blows
And thus began a war of worlds.

The climate changed, requiring clothes,
Danger stalked the flowered glen,
So their open circle began to close,
At the beginning of the Age of Men.

They then built houses all in rows,
With towers and walls of rugged stone,
Surrounded by moats that would enclose,
The gentle when they were alone.

Then writing books of rhyme and prose,
They etched their knowledge down in clay,
So in time they could expose
Future generations to their way.

And from that time their river flows,
A stream of liquid joy and love,
A message that in the darkness glows,
Transmitted from the Divine above.

In the final years they would compose
Epics to set our souls on fire
And light the lamp each pilgrim knows,
To warm them with its pure desire.

This is the destiny we chose,
To incarnate in matter's strife,
To face the battle and expose
The deepest meanings of our life.

We are divinity in the throes,
Of an epic battle for our soul,
We are the reincarnated rose,
Growing up from matter's hole.

And the secret they left is: "Live with Eros,"
Stand awake in the dark of night,
For we are all Eternal Heroes,
Fighting illusion to live as light.

So bend the bow of mind, expose
The lies and treachery all around,
Send forth the truth like flaming arrows,
And speak the ancient Holy Sound.

LOVE POURS FROM HIS LOTUS EYES

It was twilight once again,
So the restless stars were winking,
Trying to get our attention:
"Look up here without blinking,

O lost and lazy mortals,
We are the shining guardians,
Of unseen cosmic portals,
The protectors of those bastions."

But eons passed in stony silence
And the crushing depredations,
Wrought their mindless violence,
Burning libraries and nations.

Until the planets held a council,
Standing together in the sky,
Focusing their common will,
On Eternal Truth that will not die.

Then from His slumber Vishnu awoke,
There in eternal paradise,
He glanced across the blinding smoke
And love poured from His lotus eyes.

Love in the form of blazing spirits,
Streaked toward the Earth aflame,
Racing through the night like comets,
In concert chanting His Holy Names.

Striking the world in unison,
They reached the waiting wombs,
Of mothers, praying for daughters and sons,
Who would bring light into the tomb.

Unseen, unheard, those Angels dove,
Into the swirling earthly fray,
Holding the wish of eternal love,
Shining their light, to show the way.

Down, down, down to the depths of matter,
Scattered across the globe in every place,
To the bottom of the celestial ladder,
In human bodies, they hid their grace.

And in those bodies cut and torn,
They were wounded and abused,
With the pains every savior has borne,
They suffered their divinity unused.

For coming into matter they had forgotten,
The sacred mission on which they were sent,
The holy task for which they were begotten,
The eternal purpose for which they were meant.

But now is the time, O children of delight,
To drive away the demons of doubt and fear,
To stand again and shine your truth and light,
To speak that truth to every ear.

LOVE POURS FROM HIS LOTUS EYES CONT'D

And when they did the darkness faded,
Like mist before the rising Sun,
Peace returned where love invaded,
Every child was safe and all were one.

Calling all Angels, now is the time
To show the light you have come to bear.
Devas awake again to shine
And broadcast this message everywhere.

Kavindra
Mystical Poet

Jeffrey Armstrong
A Western Master of Eastern Wisdom

Award-winning author Jeffrey Armstrong (Kavindra) is a visionary motivational speaker, spiritual teacher and founder of VASA-Vedic Academy of Sciences & Arts. He is a teacher and initiate of the Vedic wisdom including Vedanta, Raja Yoga, Tantra and Mantra practices. He is also a practicing Jyotish for the past thirty-five years.

Jeffrey's first degrees were Psychology and English Literature. He studied the occult and metaphysical philosophers of all world cultures until the age of twenty-three, when he met his first guru from India, His Divine Grace A.C. Bhaktivedanta Swami Prabhupada, the founder of the International Society for Krishna Consciousness. He spent the next five years in ashrams as a celibate brahmacharya and also helped his Guru translate his various books, including the *Srimad Bhagavatam*.

In 1973, Jeffrey left the ashram and went back to University for another degree in History & Comparative Religion. After a sales career in Silicon Valley he became a corporate speaker to Fortune 500 Companies for almost ten years. At age fifty he retired from the corporate world, remarried and now, he and his wife Sandi Graham dedicate their life full time to teaching the Vedic knowledge to yoga students, ashrams and corporations around the globe.

Although a man of diverse talents, his passion is without a doubt poetry. His style is as varied as his life experiences. As a poet he has authored over a dozen books of poetry, several of which have been turned into successful musical albums. Jeffrey has been writing poetry since the age of thirteen and he now has a collection of over 1,400 poems on various subjects in many different styles. His poetry ranges from humorous and satirical to the sacred and mystical.

He is currently working on a series of six books entitled *Love Letters from a Yogi*, which describes the various flavors of mystical love. Not unlike the book you are holding in your hand, the book reveals a yogi's intimate relationship with the Divine, spoken in the ancient mystical style of Rumi, Tagore and Mirabai.

If you wish to listen to an audio version of some of his poems please go to www.JeffreyArmstrong.com or call 1-866-872-6224 for more information.